The Ultimate SOUP Cookbook

The Ultimate SOUP Cookbook

Sensational Soups for Healthy Living

Dru Melton and
Jamie Taerbaum

Inspiring | Educating | Creating | Entertaining

Brimming with creative inspiration, how-to projects, and useful information to enrich your everyday life, Quarto Knows is a favorite destination for those pursuing their interests and passions. Visit our site and dig deeper with our books into your area of interest: Quarto Creates, Quarto Cooks, Quarto Homes, Quarto Lives, Quarto Drives, Quarto Explores, Quarto Gifts, or Quarto Kids.

This edition published in 2020 by Crestline,
an imprint of The Quarto Group
142 West 36th Street, 4th Floor
New York, NY 10018 USA
T (212) 779-4972 F (212) 779-6058
www.QuartoKnows.com

First published in 2012 by Race Point Publishing, an imprint of The Quarto Group,
142 West 36th Street, 4th Floor, New York, NY, 10018, USA.

Crestline titles are also available at discount for retail, wholesale, promotional, and bulk purchase. For details, contact the Special Sales Manager by email at specialsales@quarto.com or by mail at The Quarto Group, Attn: Special Sales-Manager, 100 Cummings Center, Suite 265-D, Beverly, MA 01915, USA.

Photography by Bill Bettencourt
Food styling by Lynne Aloia

10 9 8 7 6 5 4

ISBN: 978-0-7858-3891-3

Printed in China TT012021

Previously published as *The Soupbox Cookbook*

CONTENTS

INTRODUCTION   8

CHAPTER ONE
VA VA VEGETABLES   11

CHAPTER TWO
SAUSAGE, BACON, BEEF, AND OTHER MEATY FLAVORS   61

CHAPTER THREE
CHICKEN AND OTHER FEATHERED FRIENDS   89

CHAPTER FOUR
CREAMY, CHEESY OR TOMATO-Y SOUPS, AND BISQUES   123

CHAPTER FIVE
FANTASTIC FISH, SEAFOOD, AND OTHER HEARTY CHOWDERS   145

CHAPTER SIX

HEARTY STEWS AND CHILIS FROM ALL OVER THE MAP   175

CHAPTER SEVEN

LIGHT, WARM-WEATHER SOUPS   211

CHAPTER EIGHT

A WORD ON STOCK   225

ABOUT THE AUTHORS   232
ACKNOWLEDGEMENTS   233
RECIPE INDEX   234
INDEX   237

INTRODUCTION

Ahh soup. How to describe something with so many personal meanings and interpretations? Soup is something familiar to everyone. Soup is served everywhere. Everyone remembers a few choice soups from a favorite restaurant, vacation or meal at a relative's house. Soup is more than food. It's friendly. It's a joy.

Soup transports people back in time. It takes us to Grandma's kitchen, our childhood home, happy places. It fills the house with good, rich, and appealing smells. It's homey, something made with love, full of flavor, and the memories of the people who made it. We eat soup for special occasions, fancy meals as well as sickness or when we run out of money. From quick and simple broths to rich and time-consuming stews and chowders, soup satisfies with great flavors, transforming simple water to pure bliss. Soup is the one-size-fits-all dish that's capable of satisfying many palates at once.

For many, soup can mean "comfort." In more words, it can mean, "Home. Satisfaction. Nutritious and nurturing." It can be highbrow and low end, sometimes at the same time; glamorous or humble depending on your whim. The right soup can brighten your day. Soup is equally at home as a first course or an entrée; few other foods can lay the same claim.

Soup means so many things to so many people for good reason. Soup brings a home cook or a professional chef easy and quick means to a satisfying end; that special moment when the spoon hits the tongue and the face brightens with a smile.

CHAPTER ONE

VA VA VEGETABLES

To cook a great vegetable soup you need to pay careful attention to the aromatics, the carrots, celery, onion, garlic, and spices. A good soup is like a good house, you have to build it from the foundation. Make sure you sauté the aromatics carefully and wait until you bring out the fragrance which will flavor the oil and create that flavor foundation.

The great thing about soup is its simplicity. You could take all the ingredients for any of the recipes, throw them into a pot and 30 to 50 minutes later you'll get soup. However, if you introduce the onions, celery, carrots or whatever you are starting with to heated oil or butter, and cook until translucent, you release great tasting oils that add big flavor. Heat transforms the taste; if you bite into a raw onion, it tastes bright and sharp, but if you slowly sauté it, you can make it sweet.

In the following chapter, you will find all kinds of vegetable soups for any palette. The perfect kind of broth for anyone who needs a little break from meaty soups or just merely wants a yummy dish that they can effortlessly make. The starter to your soup journey begins with a nice and tasty vegetable soup.

ROASTED BUTTERNUT SQUASH SOUP WITH SAGE AND APPLE

The sage and apple add a nice and fresh twist to this fall favorite.
This soup takes longer than most to prepare but is worth it.

Ingredients

1 butternut squash, peeled and cut into 2 inch chunks

2 medium carrots, quartered

1 medium onion, quartered

2 Gala apples, cored and peeled and cut into quarters

3 cloves garlic

2 tbsp olive or canola oil

2 bay leaves

1 tsp dried thyme

1 tsp dried sage

½ tsp salt

¼ tsp white pepper

32 oz vegetable stock

1 cup heavy cream

Cooking Instructions

Preheat the oven to 425 degrees. In a large mixing bowl toss the squash, carrots, onion, apples, garlic and the dried herbs in the olive oil and spread them evenly on a foil-lined baking sheet. Roast in the oven until the squash is tender, approximately 35-45 minutes. The vegetables should be tender and lightly browned. Remove them from the oven and transfer the contents of the baking sheet to a large stockpot set over medium heat.

Add the vegetable stock, bring the contents to a simmer and cook for 15 minutes to allow the flavors to marry. After 15 minutes, remove the soup from the heat and purée with a food processor in batches. If the soup is too thick, add a bit more stock. Add the heavy cream. (Be sure to remove from heat first.) Taste the soup and adjust seasonings with salt and pepper as needed.

Serves 6 | PREP TIME: 30 minutes. COOK TIME: 1½ hours.

MUSHROOM BARLEY SOUP

Ingredients

8 oz or one cup white button mushrooms, sliced

8 oz or one cup shitake mushrooms, sliced

1 medium onion, diced

1 medium carrot, diced

2 stalks celery, diced

2 tbsp olive oil

2 cloves garlic, minced

1 tsp thyme

2 bay leaves

48 oz vegetable stock

½ cup pearled barley

Salt and fresh ground pepper to taste

VEGAN FAVORITE

Cooking Instructions

In a large stockpot with a lid, sweat the mushrooms, onion, carrot, and celery in the olive oil over medium heat for 10 minutes. Stir often. Add the garlic, thyme and bay leaves and cook till fragrant, about one minute longer. Add the vegetable stock, cover and bring the soup to a simmer. Add the pearled barley and cook for 35-45 minutes until the barley is tender. Taste and adjust seasoning with salt and pepper if needed.

Serves 8 | PREP TIME: 10 minutes. COOK TIME: 50 minutes.

FIRE-ROASTED VEGETABLE SOUP

This can be a family favorite during the summer. If you grill a lot, you can make this soup with leftovers—it's a great way to make sure nothing is wasted and also very yummy and healthy for you, too!

Ingredients

2 large zucchini, halved

2 large yellow summer squash, halved

1 large red onion, cut into ½ inch slices

2 large carrots, quartered

1 large red pepper, halved

6 mushrooms, skewered

1 tbsp olive oil

½ tsp salt

½ tsp garlic powder

½ tsp oregano

¼ tsp freshly ground black pepper

1 shallot, minced

2 cloves garlic, minced

2 medium tomatoes, chopped

32 oz vegetable stock

½ cup acini di pepe pasta

1 tbsp butter

Cooking Instructions

Light a grill and rake the hot coals to one side. Spray or rub the zucchini, yellow squash, red onion, carrots, red pepper and mushrooms with the olive oil and then sprinkle with the spices. Grill the vegetables until just tender and a little bit charred on all sides, turning carefully as they cook, about 5-10 minutes. A grilling basket can be used if you prefer.

Once the vegetables are done remove to a plate and allow to cool. Sauté the minced shallot in a large stockpot set over medium heat until fragrant, about 5 minutes. Add the garlic to the pot and cook for one minute, stirring constantly. Add the chopped tomatoes and the stock to the pot and bring the soup to a simmer.

Now that the soup is simmering, chop the grilled vegetables into ½ inch chunks. Add them to the soup along with the acini di pepe pasta and cook until the pasta is al dente, about 6 minutes. Taste the soup and adjust seasonings as necessary with salt and pepper.

VEGAN FAVORITE

Serves 4-6 | PREP TIME: 10 minutes. COOK TIME: 45 minutes.

SEVEN-BEAN MÉLANGE

Mélange is French for mix and the combination of different beans gives this dish its unique flavor and texture. The recipe is easy to prepare, very hearty as well as being healthy for you. You can substitute different kinds of beans if desired or more convenient.

Ingredients

½ cup dry navy beans
½ cup dry pinto beans
½ cup dry chick peas
½ cup dry dark red kidney beans
½ cup dry Great Northern white beans
½ cup black-eyed peas
½ cup red lentils
1 medium red onion, diced
2 medium carrots, sliced
2 stalks celery, diced
2 cloves garlic, minced
1 tbsp tomato paste
½ tsp marjoram
¼ tsp thyme
½ tsp salt
¼ tsp freshly ground black pepper
32 oz vegetable stock
½ tsp liquid smoke (optional)*
½ tsp fresh parsley, chopped (for garnish)
Two sprigs of scallions chopped (for garnish)

Note: You'll need to soak the beans overnight.

Cooking Instructions

The night before you plan to make this soup, soak the dry beans in 1 gallon of water with 3 tbsp kosher salt. Before you cook, drain the beans, rinse well, then use as normal.

Sauté the onion, carrot and celery in a large stockpot set over medium heat until fragrant, about 5 minutes. Add the garlic, tomato paste, marjoram, thyme, salt, pepper and parsley to the pot and cook for 2 minutes, stirring constantly. Add the stock to the pot and bring the soup to a simmer. Once the soup reaches a simmer add all the beans and cook, partially covered, until the beans are tender, about 50-60 minutes. Stir in the liquid smoke and cook for another 5 minutes. Taste the soup and adjust seasonings as necessary with salt and pepper. Garnish with some fresh parsley and chopped scallions. This can be served with toasted pita bread.

Chef's Note:

Since this recipe was designed to be vegan, we use liquid smoke in this recipe to replicate the smoked bacon/ham element that is prevalent in most bean-soup recipes. Although it can be omitted it does add a nice depth of flavor to the dish.

VEGAN
FAVORITE

Serves 6 | PREP TIME: 15 minutes. COOK TIME: 50-60 minutes.

HEARTY FRESH VEGETABLE

This is a simple and easy recipe, one that does what it should; highlights the freshest vegetables in a simple yet flavorful broth.

Ingredients

2 tbsp olive oil
1 medium yellow onion, diced
2 medium carrots, sliced
2 stalks celery, diced
2 cloves garlic, minced
2 tbsp tomato paste
½ tsp oregano
½ tsp salt
½ tsp parsley
¼ tsp freshly ground black pepper
2 tomatoes, peeled and chopped*
2 medium red skinned potatoes, diced
1 zucchini, quartered and sliced
8 oz or one cup of green beans, cut into 1 inch pieces
1 ear sweet corn, kernels cut from the cob
32 oz vegetable stock

VEGAN FAVORITE

Cooking Instructions

Sauté the onion, carrot and celery in 2 tbsp olive oil in a large stockpot set over medium heat until fragrant, about 5 minutes. Add the garlic, tomato paste, oregano, salt, pepper and parsley to the pot and cook for 2 minutes, stirring constantly. Add the vegetable stock and the chopped tomatoes to the pot and bring the soup to a simmer. Once the soup reaches a simmer add the potatoes, zucchini and green beans and cook, covered, for 20 minutes or until the potatoes are tender. Remove from the heat and stir in the corn kernels. Taste the soup and adjust seasonings as necessary with salt and pepper. Garnish with some fresh parsley and serve with crusty sour dough rolls.

Chef's Note:

To easily peel the tomatoes, cut a cross on the bottom with a sharp knife and dunk them in boiling water for a minute, then dunk them in cold water. The skin should easily peel back.

Serves 4-6 | PREP TIME: 15 minutes. COOK TIME: 30 minutes.

CALIFORNIA VEGETABLE MEDLEY SOUP

This soup is great garnished with Cheese-it crackers!

Ingredients

1 medium onion, diced
1 carrot, diced
1 large red bell pepper, diced
2 stalks celery, diced
2 tbsp butter
2 cloves garlic, minced
1 tsp dried thyme
½ tsp dried marjoram
2 bay leaves
2 pinches red pepper flakes
32 oz vegetable stock
2 large zucchini, sliced
1 cup corn kernels, fresh or frozen
1 cup milk
12 oz or 1 ½ cups white cheddar cheese, grated

Cooking Instructions

Sauté the onion, carrots, red pepper and celery in the butter over medium-low heat in a large stockpot until translucent, about 8-10 minutes. Add the garlic and herbs, and cook for 1 minute while stirring. Add the vegetable stock and bring to a simmer. Cook for 10 minutes to allow the flavors to develop. Add the zucchini and corn, and cook until the zucchini is fork tender, about 10 minutes more. Then add the milk and turn heat to low. Add the cheese a couple ounces at a time and stir constantly until incorporated. Continue until all the cheese has been added. Taste and adjust seasonings with salt and pepper as needed.

Serves 6 | PREP TIME: 10 minutes. COOK TIME: 35 minutes.

MEDITERRANEAN VEGETABLE SOUP

This light and quick soup is especially good for lunch during the summer.

Ingredients

medium onion, diced

1 medium carrot, diced

1 medium red pepper, diced

8 oz fresh mushrooms, sliced

3 tbsp olive oil

2 cloves garlic, minced

½ tsp salt

½ tsp dried oregano

½ tsp dried rosemary

½ tsp dried winter savory

1 medium eggplant, peeled and cut into 1 inch chunks

1 yellow summer squash, sliced into half moons

32 oz vegetable stock

4 oz kalamata olives, pitted and sliced

1 can artichoke bottoms, sliced

2 bay leaves

Cooking Instructions

Sauté the onion, carrot, red pepper and mushrooms in the olive oil in a large stockpot set over medium heat until the onion is translucent, about 10 minutes. Add the garlic cloves, the salt and the dried herbs and cook for one minute, stirring constantly. Add the eggplant and squash to the pot and cook for 5 minutes to develop flavor. Increase the heat to medium high and add the vegetable stock. Once the soup comes to a simmer add the olives and the artichoke bottoms. Simmer the soup for 15 minutes to allow flavors to marry. Taste the soup and adjust seasonings with salt and pepper as needed.

You can drizzle this soup with a bit of olive oil and serve it with some nice crusty bread on the side.

Serves 4 | PREP TIME: 15 minutes. COOK TIME: 35 minutes.

NORTH AFRICAN VEGETABLE SOUP

An adventurous yet simple recipe with ingredients that are easily found. This hearty vegan and gluten-free soup is easy to prepare and sure to satisfy. Garnish with chopped parsley and serve with wedges of toasted flatbread or pita.

Ingredients

1 large onion, chopped
2 carrots, sliced
1 tbsp olive oil
2 cloves garlic, minced
½ tsp salt
½ tsp cumin
½ tsp ground ginger
½ tsp tumeric
½ tsp harissa*
¼ tsp cinnamon
¼ tsp ground nutmeg
3 large tomatoes, chopped
32 oz vegetable stock
1 large sweet potato, peeled and cut into ½ inch chunks
2 small kohlrabis, peeled and cut into ½ inch chunks
2 parsnips, sliced

Cooking Instructions

Sauté the onion and the carrot in the olive oil in a large stockpot set over medium heat until fragrant, about 5 minutes. Add the garlic and spices to the pot and cook for two minutes, stirring constantly. Add the tomatoes and the stock to the pot and bring the soup to a simmer. Once a simmer is reached add the sweet potato, kohlrabi and parsnips. Cover and cook until the kohlrabi and yams are tender, about 30 minutes. Taste the soup and adjust seasonings as necessary with salt and pepper.

Chef's Note:

If you cannot find harissa (a North African chili powder spice blend) feel free to substitute ¼ tsp ground cayenne mixed with ¼ tsp ground coriander and a pinch of caraway seeds.

VEGAN FAVORITE

GLUTEN FREE

Serves 4 | PREP TIME: 10 minutes. COOK TIME: 40 minutes.

SWEET CORN CHOWDER

The most comfortable of comfort foods, thick and a great winter warmer.

Ingredients

4 medium red potatoes, washed and cut into ½ inch cubes

2 slices bacon

1 large onion, diced

2 tbsp butter

2 cloves garlic, minced

1 red bell pepper, diced

½ tsp red pepper flakes

1 tsp dried parsley

2 tbsp flour

16 oz whole milk

16 oz water

6 ears fresh sweet corn, husked and cut from the cob

Salt and pepper to taste

Cooking Instructions

Peel and cube the potatoes. Cook in a pan of boiling water for 10 minutes and then drain in a colander. While the potatoes are cooking, render the bacon over medium heat in a small skillet. When the bacon is finished, put it on paper towels to drain. Add the onion to the bacon drippings and cook for 5 minutes. Remove from heat.

Melt the butter in a stockpot over medium heat. Add the garlic and red pepper, and cook for 3 minutes, stirring constantly. Cut bacon into small pieces and add to the onions with the drippings. Add the red pepper flakes, the parsley and the flour and stir constantly for 5 minutes.

Add the milk, the water, the reserved potatoes and the corn. Heat the soup to a simmer and cook for another 20 minutes or until all the flavors have combined. Taste soup and adjust seasonings with salt or pepper.

Chef's Note:

Be sure to run the back of a knife down the cobs to extract all the corn and juice you can – there's LOTS of flavor in there!

Servings: 6 | PREP TIME: 15 minutes. COOK TIME: 35 minutes.

CUBAN BLACK BEAN SOUP

This simple and quick soup is vegan and gluten-free. The savory hint of cumin and chili powder balanced with the fresh cilantro and lime juice is a wonderful pairing.

Ingredients

1 medium onion, diced

1 medium carrot, diced

2 tbsp olive oil

½ tsp salt

2 cloves garlic, minced

2 large poblano peppers, roasted and chopped*

2 jalapeño peppers, roasted and chopped*

1 tsp cumin

½ tsp chili powder

2 cups dry black beans, soaked overnight in salted water

32 oz vegetable stock

Fresh cilantro leaves

Juice of two limes

Note: You'll need to soak the black beans overnight.

 VEGAN FAVORITE

 GLUTEN FREE

Cooking Instructions

Sauté the onion and carrot in the olive oil in a large stockpot set over medium heat until fragrant, about 5 minutes. Add the salt, garlic, roasted chiles and spices to the pot and cook for two minutes, stirring constantly. Add the beans and the stock to the pot and bring to a simmer. Cover the pot and cook until the beans are tender, about 30-40 minutes. Once the beans are tender, pulse soup in a food processor in batches to give the soup more body while leaving a lot of the beans whole. Taste the soup and adjust seasonings as necessary with salt and pepper. Garnish with fresh cilantro leaves and lime juice.

Chef's Note:

You can buy already roasted peppers in a jar. To roast the peppers in the oven, turn on the broiler, put the peppers on a broiler pan and place on the top shelf of the oven. Turn the peppers every fifteen minutes for an hour, then put in a bowl and cover with a towel to steam them a bit. Alternately you can roast them on the grill with the same approximate timing and finishing technique.

Serves 4 | PREP TIME: 10 minutes plus roasting of the peppers. COOK TIME: 45 minutes.

SPICY SOUTHWESTERN WHITE BEAN SOUP

This is another good example of a tasty, simple soup that is hearty and healthy, gluten-free and vegan. You'll be amazed at the amount of flavor packed into every bite. Garnish with scallions and serve with jalapeño corn bread and a cold beer. This is a satisfying end to a long day in the sun!

Ingredients

2 cups dry Great Northern white beans, soaked overnight in salted water

1 medium onion, diced

2 carrots, sliced

2 stalks celery, diced

2 tbsp olive oil

3 cloves garlic, minced

2 large poblano peppers, roasted and chopped*

1 serrano pepper, roasted and chopped*

1 bay leaf

½ tsp salt

½ tsp cumin

½ tsp chili powder

¼ tsp cayenne pepper

32 oz vegetable stock

Note: You'll need to soak the beans overnight.

VEGAN FAVORITE

GLUTEN FREE

Cooking Instructions

Sauté the onion, carrot and celery in the olive oil in a large stockpot set over medium heat until fragrant, about 5 minutes. Add the garlic, roasted chiles and all the spices to the pot and cook for two minutes, stirring constantly. Add the beans and stock to the pot and bring the soup to a simmer. Once a simmer is reached cover the pot and cook until the beans are tender, about 30-40 minutes. Once the beans are tender pulse in a food processor in batches to a thick but not quite smooth consistency. Taste the soup and adjust seasonings as necessary with salt and pepper.

Chef's Note:

As with the Cuban black-bean soup, you can buy already roasted peppers in a jar. To roast the peppers at home, turn on the broiler, put the peppers on a broiler pan and place on the top shelf of the oven. Turn the peppers every fifteen minutes for an hour, then put in a bowl and cover with a towel to steam them a bit. Alternately you can roast them on the grill with the same approximate timing and finishing technique.

Serves 4 | PREP TIME: 10 minutes plus roasting of the peppers. COOK TIME: 45 minutes.

WEST INDIAN SQUASH SAMBAR

Ingrediants

1 acorn or Hubbard squash, roasted, peeled and cut into 1 inch chunks

1 large onion, diced

2 carrots, sliced

2 tbsp olive oil

2 cloves garlic, minced

1 tsp salt

½ tsp cumin

½ tsp red curry powder

½ tsp turmeric

½ tsp cayenne pepper

1 jalapeño pepper, seeded and diced

32 oz vegetable stock

1 cup red lentils

4 oz coconut milk

Salt and pepper to taste

Cooking Instructions

Roast the whole squash in a 400-degree oven for 30 minutes. Remove and allow to cool, then peel and chop the squash and set aside. Prepare the rest of the soup while the squash roasts.

Warm the oil in a stockpot over medium heat. Add the onion and carrot and sauté until softened, about 10 minutes. Add the garlic and the dry spices, and cook until fragrant, about one minute. Add the jalapeño pepper and the vegetable stock. Bring to a simmer and cook for 10 minutes. Add the lentils and the squash, and cook another 15 minutes to allow the lentils to soften and the flavors to develop. When the lentils and the squash are tender remove the soup from heat and add the coconut milk. Taste and add salt and pepper as needed.

VEGAN FAVORITE

GLUTEN FREE

Serves 6 | PREP TIME: 15 minutes. COOK TIME: 40-45 minutes.

WHITE BEAN & ESCAROLE SOUP

This is a take on a classic Italian recipe.
Kale is a great substitute if you can't find escarole.

Ingredients

1 lb cannellini or Great Northern white beans, soaked overnight

4 oz pancetta or bacon, chopped

1 medium onion, diced

1 medium carrot, diced

1 stalk celery, diced

½ tsp dried oregano

¼ tsp dried marjoram

¼ tsp dried thyme

½ tsp salt

2 bay leaves

Pinch red pepper flakes

2 cloves garlic, minced

32 oz chicken or vegetable stock

1 head escarole, washed and cut into ribbons (tough stems removed)*

Salt and pepper to taste

Cooking Instructions

Cook the pancetta or bacon in a large stockpot over medium heat to render the fat, about 5 minutes. Add the onion, carrot and celery to the stockpot and cook over medium heat until translucent, about 10 minutes. Add the dried herbs, salt, pepper and garlic and cook for one minute, stirring constantly. Add the stock and the beans, and bring the soup to a simmer. Once the soup has reached a simmer cook for 20-30 minutes until the beans are tender, stirring occasionally. Once the beans are tender add the escarole and cook for another 15 minutes. Use the flat of a spatula to smash a few beans against the side of the stockpot to give the soup some extra body and a smoother texture. Taste the soup and adjust seasonings with salt and pepper as needed.

Chef's Note:

Escarole isn't available in many markets, so feel free to substitute kale or collard or mustard greens, all of which will taste great in this soup.

Serves 6 | PREP TIME: 15 minutes. COOK TIME: 30 minutes.

SPLIT-PEA SOUP

A traditional favorite.

Ingredients

16 oz dried split peas
2 tablespoons butter
1 cup onions diced
1 cup carrots diced
1 tablespoon minced garlic
16 oz smoked ham cut into half inch cubes
8 cups chicken stock
1 bay leaf
Salt and pepper to taste

Note: You'll need to soak the split peas for at least 8 hours ahead of time, or bring to a boil and let rest for an hour.

Cooking Instructions

Place the peas in a large pot or bowl, cover with water by 2 inches and soak 8 hours or overnight. Drain the peas and set aside. Alternately cover the peas with water and bring to a boil, then turn off the stove and let them rest for an hour before proceeding with the recipe.

In a large pot, melt the butter over medium-high heat. Add the onions and carrots and cook, stirring, for 5 minutes. Add the garlic and cook, stirring, for 1 minute. Add the ham and cook for another 5 minutes. Add the stock, the bay leaf, the drained peas and a pinch of salt and cook, stirring occasionally, until the peas are tender, about 1½ hours. Add more water as needed, if the soup becomes too thick or dry. Remove the bay leaf and discard. Season with salt and pepper to taste. Serve immediately.

Serves 8 | PREP TIME: 20 minutes. COOK TIME: 1½ hours.

YELLOW SPLIT-PEA SOUP WITH FENNEL

This soup warms the soul and is the perfect accompaniment to a good book
and your favorite blanket. Try it garnished with croutons or popcorn for a unique finish.

Ingredients

1 medium onion, diced

1 carrot, diced

2 stalks celery, diced

1 tbsp olive oil

2 cloves garlic, minced

1 small bulb of fennel, sliced (reserve the stalks and fronds for another use)

½ tsp salt

¼ tsp thyme

¼ tsp white pepper

1 lb yellow split peas, picked over to remove shriveled or broken peas, and rinsed

32 oz vegetable stock

Salt and pepper to taste

Cooking Instructions

Sauté the onion, carrots and celery in the olive oil in a large stockpot set over medium heat until fragrant, about 5 minutes. Add the garlic, fennel and spices to the pot and cook for two minutes, stirring constantly. Add the yellow spilt peas and the stock to the pot and bring the soup to a simmer. Once a simmer is reached, cover the pot, turn heat to low and cook until the split peas are just tender, about 30-40 minutes. Once the peas are tender pulse briefly with an immersion blender (or in batches in a food processor) to give the soup a bit more body and texture. Taste the soup and adjust seasonings as necessary with salt and pepper.

Serves 4-6 | PREP TIME: 15 minutes. COOK TIME: 45 minutes.

LENTIL SOUP WITH LEMON

This is a quick and light soup that's great all year round. The contrast between the savory tomato paste and the creamy lentils is highlighted by a splash of lemon juice added at the end of cooking. Served with a nice salad, this recipe is a delicious and healthy lunch.

Ingredients

1 medium onion, diced

2 carrots, sliced

2 stalks celery, diced

1 tbsp olive oil

½ tsp salt

2 cloves garlic, minced

2 tbsp tomato paste

¼ tsp dried thyme

¼ tsp chervil

¼ tsp marjoram

2 tomatoes, chopped

1 lb green lentils, picked over to remove shriveled or broken lentils, and rinsed

32 oz vegetable stock

1 small zucchini, cut into half moons

Juice of two lemons

Salt and pepper to taste

Cooking Instructions

Sauté the onion, carrots and celery in the olive oil in a large stockpot set over medium heat until fragrant, about 5 minutes. Add the salt, garlic, the tomato paste and dried spices to the pot and cook for two minutes, stirring constantly. Add the tomatoes, lentils and the stock to the pot and bring the soup to a simmer. Cover the pot, and cook until the lentils are tender, about 20 minutes. Once the lentils are tender pulse briefly with an immersion blender (or take a small batch and pulse in a food processor and return to the soup) to give the soup a bit more body and texture. Add the zucchini and cook until just tender, about 5 minutes longer. Remove from the heat and stir in the lemon juice. Taste the soup and adjust seasonings as necessary with salt and pepper.

VEGAN
FAVORITE

GLUTEN
FREE

Serves 4-6 | PREP TIME: 10 minutes. COOK TIME: 30 minutes.

MASALA TOMATO LENTIL

Masala refers to a special spice paste with flavors from the Far East. There are a lot of steps in the cooking process, but the rewards are evident in the bowl.

Ingredients

3 large tomatoes, halved
2 tbsp olive oil

3 cloves garlic, smashed
1 one inch piece of ginger, peeled and grated
1 tbsp garam masala spice blend
1 tsp red curry powder
½ tsp turmeric
¼ tsp cinnamon
¼ tsp cloves
½ tsp salt
½ tsp cumin

1 medium onion, diced
2 carrots, diced
2 stalks celery, diced
2 cups red lentils, picked over to remove shriveled and broken beans, and rinsed
32 oz vegetable stock
Salt and pepper to taste*

Cooking Instructions

Preheat the oven to 325 degrees. Drizzle the halved tomatoes with olive oil and sprinkle them with salt. Place them skin side down on a foil-lined baking sheet and roast in the oven for 90 minutes.

Make the masala spice paste and the rest of the soup while the tomatoes roast. Place the smashed cloves of garlic and the grated ginger in a mortar. Add the dry spices and mash everything together in the mortar until it becomes a rough paste. You should have about 1-2 tablespoons. Set aside.

Sauté the onion, carrot and celery in the remaining olive oil (about 1 tbsp) in a large stockpot set over medium heat until fragrant, about 5 minutes. Add the garlic and masala paste to the pot and cook for one minute, stirring constantly. Add the lentils and the stock to the pot and bring the soup to a simmer. Once a simmer is reached cover the pot and cook until the lentils are tender, about 20-25 minutes. When the tomatoes are done, pull them from the oven and add them to the soup. Pulse with an immersion blender (or pulse in your food processor in batches) to the desired consistency, making sure there are a few chunks left for texture. Taste the soup and adjust seasonings as necessary with salt and pepper.

VEGAN FAVORITE

GLUTEN FREE

Chef's Note:

Often times, especially when there are strong spices, home chefs under-salt their soups. This is fine if you want to reduce salt in your diet. But if you aren't going low sodium, and your soup isn't coming out perfectly, try adding ½ teaspoon salt or more.

Serves 4-6 | PREP TIME: 20 minutes. COOK TIME: 1 hour 45 minutes.

ROASTED CARROT & FENNEL SOUP

Fennel is a great counterpoint to the sweetness of carrots, making an appealing and balanced flavor combination to serve guests. If your significant other's parents are coming to dinner, this is the perfect soup to serve; It's complex and different but not difficult to make.

Ingredients

1 large bulb fennel, sliced (reserve some of the fronds for garnish)

6 large carrots, cut into 1 inch chunks

1 large onion, quartered

2 stalks celery, cut into 1 inch chunks

2 tbsp olive oil

1 tsp salt

½ tsp sugar

1 head of garlic, wrapped in foil

32 oz vegetable stock

1 tsp dried thyme

2 bay leaves

Salt and pepper to taste

Cooking Instructions

Preheat the oven to 375 degrees. Line a baking sheet with foil. Toss the fennel, carrots, onion and celery with the oil, salt and sugar, and place the vegetables on the baking sheet along with the head of garlic in foil. Roast in the oven for 30-40 minutes until soft, turning the vegetables a couple times so they cook evenly. While the vegetables roast, add the stock and the dried herbs to a large pot and keep warm on low heat. Once the vegetables are browned and soft, remove from the oven and add them to the warmed stock. Remove the bay leaves and purée the soup with an immersion blender (or food processor in batches) until the soup is thick and almost smooth. Taste and adjust seasonings with salt and pepper as needed.

VEGAN FAVORITE

GLUTEN FREE

Serves 6 | PREP TIME: 10 minutes. COOK TIME: 45 minutes.

BIRTHDAY SOUP

Ingredients

4 medium carrots, sliced

2 stalks celery, small diced

1 small onion, small diced

1 clove garlic, minced

2 bay leaves

1 tsp dried thyme

1 tsp dried parsley

½ tsp dried marjoram

32 oz vegetable stock

3 fresh tomatoes, diced (or one 14.5 ounce canned diced tomatoes)

½ tsp salt

1 cup fresh or frozen peas

2 large potatoes, medium diced

6 oz rotini pasta

Salt and pepper to taste

Cooking Instructions

Sauté the carrots, celery and onion in a stockpot over medium heat until translucent; about 10 minutes. Add the garlic and the dried herbs and cook for one minute. Add the vegetable stock, the tomatoes and the salt and bring to a simmer, stirring occasionally. Once the soup has reached a simmer, add the peas, potatoes and pasta, and cook until tender, approximately 20 minutes. Taste the soup and adjust seasonings with salt and pepper as needed.

Chef's Note:

You can add potatoes and noodles in your soup. The rotini can be omitted easily enough to make this gluten-free. Just add another potato to maintain the heartiness of the dish.

VEGAN FAVORITE

GLUTEN FREE*

*Can be made gluten free by omitting the pasta and adding another potato.

Serves 6 | PREP TIME: 10 minutes. COOK TIME: 35 minutes.

ROASTED CARROT & GINGER BISQUE

Roasting the vegetables brings out the natural sugars while the ginger adds a touch of heat for a nice flavor twist. This soup is versatile enough to stand as an entrée or a lunch, and is easy to make.

Ingredients

1 lb carrots, cut into chunks
1 large sweet potato, peeled and quartered
1 medium onion, quartered
1 clove garlic, smashed
32 oz vegetable stock
1 tbsp grated fresh ginger
1 tbsp olive oil
1 bay leaf
½ tsp salt
½ tsp granulated sugar
¼ tsp white pepper

Cooking Instructions

Preheat the oven to 400 degrees. Toss the carrots, sweet potato and onion with the salt and the sugar in the olive oil and turn out onto a foil lined baking sheet. Roast uncovered in the oven for 20 minutes or until caramelized. Remove from the oven and add the vegetables and vegetable stock to a large pot set over medium heat. Add the ginger, garlic and white pepper and bring the soup to a simmer. Once a simmer is reached turn the heat to low and cook for 10 minutes until the flavors marry. Remove from the heat and pulse with an immersion blender to desired consistency. Taste the soup and adjust seasonings as necessary with salt and pepper. Garnish with fresh parsley.

VEGAN FAVORITE

GLUTEN FREE

Serves 4 | PREP TIME: 10 minutes. COOK TIME: 35 minutes

SAVORY CREAM OF ASPARAGUS

One of Spring's first vegetables to appear, asparagus is great on the grill and in salads, but also shines in a soup like this. It's quick to make and freezes well.

Ingredients

4 tbsp butter
2 shallots, diced
3 tbsp flour
1 clove garlic, minced
½ tsp salt
¼ tsp black pepper
16 oz vegetable or chicken stock
16 oz milk
1 lb asparagus, washed and cut into 1 inch pieces
1 cup heavy cream
Salt and pepper to taste

Cooking Instructions

Melt the butter in a large stockpot over medium heat. Sauté the shallots in the butter until fragrant, about 5 minutes. Add the flour and cook for 3 minutes, stirring constantly. Add the garlic, salt and pepper to the pot and cook for 2 minutes more, stirring constantly. Add the stock and the milk, and bring to a slow simmer, stirring regularly. The soup will finish thickening shortly after a simmer is reached, about 10 minutes. Add the asparagus pieces and cook until tender, about 10 minutes longer. Once the asparagus is tender, you can remove some of the pieces to use to garnish. Pulse the soup with an immersion blender (or food processor in batches) until smooth. Return the purée to the pot, remove from heat and stir in the heavy cream. Taste the soup and adjust seasonings as necessary with salt and pepper. Garnish with reserved asparagus pieces and serve.

Serves 4 | PREP TIME: 15 minutes. COOK TIME: 30 minutes

FRESH TOMATO & BASIL BISQUE

Our take on a classic tomato soup. It's a homerun with the roasted tomatoes combined with the light garlic flavor.

Ingredients

1 medium onion, ¼ inch diced

2 medium carrots, ¼ inch diced

2 tbsp butter

2 cloves garlic, minced

2 lbs fresh tomatoes, peeled and seeded (we use Roma tomatoes)

24 oz vegetable stock

1 cup heavy cream

1 cup fresh basil leaves, cut into chiffonade (long thin strips done by folding the leaves or rolling them before cutting them)

Salt and fresh ground pepper to taste

GLUTEN FREE

Cooking Instructions

Sauté the onion and carrots in the butter over medium heat in a large stockpot until translucent, about 10 minutes. Add the garlic and cook two minutes longer. Add the tomatoes and cook for 10 minutes, breaking them up with a spatula as they cook. Add the vegetable stock and bring the soup to a simmer. Simmer for 5 minutes to allow the flavors to marry. Remove the soup from the heat and process with an immersion blender (or food processor in batches) until smooth. Add the heavy cream and basil leaves. Taste and adjust seasonings as needed with salt and pepper.

Chef's Note:

You can garnish this with a spoonful of mascarpone cheese right before you serve it.

Serves 6 | PREP TIME: 15 minutes. COOK TIME: 40-45 minutes.

SUN-DRIED TOMATO & ROASTED GARLIC SOUP

This soup is like the Tomato Basil Bisque's sophisticated cousin.
The sun-dried tomatoes add deeper flavor to the dish.

Ingredients

1 medium onion, diced

1 medium carrot, diced

1 stalk celery, diced

2 tbsp olive oil

2 bay leaves

½ tsp dried oregano

½ tsp dried basil

½ tsp salt

¼ tsp white pepper

1 head garlic, roasted and mashed (divided)

32 oz chicken stock

2 lbs fresh tomatoes, peeled seeded and diced

6 oz sun dried tomatoes, chopped

1 cup heavy cream

Salt and pepper to taste

Cooking Instructions

Sauté the onion, carrot and celery in the olive oil in a large stockpot over medium heat until translucent, about 10 minutes. Add the dried herbs, salt, pepper and half of the roasted garlic and cook for one minute, stirring constantly. Add the chicken stock and the fresh tomatoes and bring the soup to a simmer. Once the soup has reached a simmer, cook for another 15 minutes to allow the flavor to develop. Purée the soup with an immersion blender until smooth. Add the sun-dried tomatoes and the rest of the mashed garlic, and remove from the heat. Stir in the heavy cream. Taste the soup and adjust seasonings with salt and pepper as needed.

GLUTEN
FREE

Serves 6 | PREP TIME: 10 minutes. COOK TIME: 50 minutes.

TOMATO FLORENTINE SOUP

An easy to make and heartier soup that eats like a meal.

Ingrediants

12 oz uncooked sweet Italian sausage, crumbled

1 medium onion, small dice

1 stalk celery, small dice

1 medium carrot, small dice

2 tablespoons olive oil

2 cloves garlic, minced

4 cups fresh tomatoes or 2 (14.5 ounce) cans diced tomatoes

1 (14.5 ounce) can tomato sauce

32 oz homemade stock or canned beef broth

1 tsp dried basil

1 tsp dried thyme

1 tsp dried oregano

2 bay leaves

1 bunch fresh spinach, washed & chopped or one box frozen chopped spinach thawed and drained

1 cup pasta shells

Salt and pepper to taste

Cooking Instructions

Warm a saucepan over medium heat. Add 1 tablespoon of the oil and cook the sausage, onion, celery and carrot over medium heat until the meat is no longer pink. Drain. Stir in the other tablespoon of oil, the garlic, tomatoes, stock, tomato sauce, basil, thyme, oregano and bay leaves. Bring to a boil. Reduce heat; cover and simmer for 10 minutes. Add the spinach and the pasta shells and cook for another 10-15 minutes to allow the shells to cook and the flavors to meld. Taste the soup and adjust with salt and pepper as needed. Serve immediately.

Chef's Note:

To roast the garlic, preheat the oven to 400 degrees. Peel away the outer layer of the garlic's skin. Cut the top off the whole clove of garlic so each individual clove is cut. Pour a teaspoon of oil over the clove (or cloves if you want to cook more and save some for other uses). Put the clove or cloves on a baking sheet and cover with aluminum foil. Roast for 30 minutes. The cloves should be browned and soft all the way through. When cool, use a small fork to remove the cloves or squeeze each one out. Mmmmm, good in this soup, on toast or both!

Serves 4 | PREP TIME: 20 minutes. COOK TIME: 45 minutes.

MULLIGATAWNY SOUP

The name of this fantastic British and Indian creation means 'pepper water.'

Ingredients

1 large red onion, diced
2 stalks of celery, diced (leaves included)
1 carrot, diced
1 tbsp olive oil
1 tbsp butter
1 lb chicken breast, cubed
2 cloves garlic, minced
½ tsp salt
1 tbsp curry powder
½ tsp cumin
¼ tsp cinnamon
¼ tsp clove
¼ tsp turmeric
¼ tsp white pepper
32 oz chicken stock
1 cup red lentils
1 granny smith apple, peeled, cored and diced
½ cup heavy cream
Salt and pepper to taste
Fresh cilantro for garnish

GLUTEN FREE

Cooking Instructions

Melt the butter with the olive oil in a large stockpot over medium hot. Sauté the onion, celery and carrot in the olive oil until translucent, about 8 minutes. Add the chicken and cook until done, about 10 minutes. Add the garlic, salt, curry powder, cumin, cinnamon, clove, turmeric and white pepper to the pot and cook for two minutes, stirring constantly. Add the stock, lentils and diced apple to the pot and bring to a simmer. Once the soup reaches a simmer cover the pot, turn heat to low and cook for 20 minutes until the lentils are done. Taste and adjust seasonings as necessary with salt and pepper. Remove from heat and stir in the heavy cream. Garnish with fresh cilantro. This goes well served with rice but can be eaten on its own, too.

Serves 4-6 | PREP TIME: 10 minutes. COOK TIME: 20 minutes.

STUFFED GREEN PEPPER SOUP

Ingredients

1 lb ground sirloin

2 large green peppers, chopped

2 cloves garlic, minced

3 fresh roma tomatoes, seeded and chopped or one 14.5 oz can diced tomatoes

1 small onion, small dice

1 stalk celery, small dice

48 oz beef stock

2 oz tomato paste

1 tsp dried thyme

½ tsp freshly ground black pepper

2 tbsp soy sauce

1 tbsp brown sugar

1 cup white or basmati rice

Salt and pepper to taste

Cooking Instructions

Brown the ground beef with the onion and celery in a large stockpot over medium heat. Drain well. Add the green peppers, garlic and tomatoes and return to heat. Add the onion and cook on medium heat for 5 minutes to allow flavors to develop. Add the beef stock, tomato paste, thyme, pepper, soy sauce and the brown sugar and bring soup to a simmer. Once the soup reaches a simmer add the rice and cook till the rice is done, about 20 minutes. Taste the soup and adjust seasonings with salt and pepper as needed.

Serves 4 | PREP TIME: 20 minutes. COOK TIME: 35 minutes.

BROCCOLI RABE SOUP WITH LENTILS & SPRING ONIONS

Broccoli rabe (also known as rapini) is a wild form of the traditional broccoli we know and love. It forms smaller heads than regular broccoli, but the stems and leaves can also be used and are delicious. Here the broccoli rabe is nicely paired with earthy lentils and spring onions. This simple soup is a joy to serve and eat.

Ingredients

3 spring onions, diced (you can substitute any other sweet onion)

2 carrots, chopped

2 stalks celery, sliced

2 tbsp butter

1 lb broccoli rabe, washed and cut into 1-inch lengths (leaves included)

2 cloves garlic, minced

1 pinch red pepper flakes

1 tsp thyme

½ tsp marjoram

1 bay leaf

1 cup green lentils, rinsed and picked over

1 tbsp tomato paste

48 oz vegetable stock

1 tsp lemon zest, minced

Cooking Instructions

Set a 4-quart stockpot on high heat with one inch of water and a steamer basket set inside. Sauté the onion, carrots and celery in the butter over medium low heat in another large stockpot until translucent, about 8-10 minutes.

While the aromatics are cooking, steam the broccoli rabe for 10 minutes.

Add the garlic, the pepper flakes and the herbs to the pot with the aromatics. Cook for 1 minute, stirring constantly. Add the lentils, tomato paste and vegetable stock. Bring to a simmer, cover and turn heat to low. Cook for 20-25 minutes until the lentils are soft and the flavors have developed. Add the lemon zest. Taste and adjust seasonings with salt and pepper as needed.

Chef's Note:

Spring onions are onions picked before they get a chance to form bulbs. Normally, they are a bit sweeter than regular onions. They can be found in farmers' markets in May and June. Also, steaming the broccoli rabe before adding it to the soup (rather than just dropping it into the soup) is a good idea because of this vegetable's strong taste—it's a bitter green after all. Steaming takes out some of the bitterness and gives it a nice mellow flavor.

Serves 6 | PREP TIME: 10 minutes. COOK TIME: 25 minutes.

GREEN BEAN & ZUCCHINI SOUP WITH QUINOA

The bacon and farm-fresh vegetables are an unbeatable combination. Add tasty quinoa, one of the few vegetables that contains all nine of the essential amino acids for your body, and it's healthy to boot, a win-win. You can serve this soup with hearty toasted pumpernickel bread.

Ingredients

4 oz bacon, cut into ½ inch squares

1 medium yellow onion, diced

2 medium carrots, sliced

2 stalks celery, diced

1 tbsp canola oil

2 cloves garlic, minced

2 tbsp tomato paste

½ tsp dried thyme

½ tsp salt

½ tsp freshly ground black pepper

½ tsp dried parsley

2 tomatoes, peeled and chopped

32 oz vegetable stock

12 oz green beans, cut into 1-inch pieces

2 zucchinis, quartered and sliced in ¼ inch pieces

1 cup quinoa

Salt and pepper to taste

Parsley, chopped for garnish

GLUTEN FREE

Cooking Instructions

Sauté the bacon with the onion, carrot and celery in the canola oil in a large stockpot set over medium heat until fragrant, about 5 minutes. Add the garlic, tomato paste, thyme, salt, pepper and parsley, and cook for one minute, stirring constantly. Add the tomatoes and stock. Bring to a simmer and add the green beans, zucchini and quinoa. Cover and cook for 20 minutes until the beans are tender and the quinoa is done. Taste the soup and adjust seasonings as necessary with salt and pepper. Garnish with fresh parsley.

Serves 6 | PREP TIME: 15 minutes. COOK TIME: 30 minutes.

VEGETABLE SOUP

This hearty and satisfying soup is perfect for an early winter bounty. If there ever was a soup that went perfectly in a sourdough bread bowl, this is the one.

Ingredients

1 large onion, diced
2 carrots, sliced
2 stalks celery, sliced
2 tbsp canola oil
2 garlic cloves, minced
1 tsp dried thyme
1 tsp salt
1 tsp black pepper
1 tsp dried rosemary
1 tsp dried marjoram
1 tsp dried parsley
48 oz vegetable stock
1 small bulb of fennel, sliced
2 parsnips, sliced
2 medium turnips, peeled and diced
2 medium red potatoes, peeled and diced
1 bunch of kale, stemmed and cut into strips
Salt and pepper to taste
Fresh parsley, chopped for garnish
Parmesan shavings for garnish

Cooking Instructions

Sauté the onion, carrot and celery in the canola oil in a large stockpot set over medium heat until fragrant, about 5 minutes. Add the garlic, thyme, salt, pepper, rosemary, marjoram and parsley and cook for one minute, stirring constantly. Add the stock and bring to a simmer. Add the fennel, parsnips, turnips, potatoes and kale. Cover and cook for 30-40 minutes or until the parsnip and potatoes are tender. Taste the soup and adjust seasonings as necessary with salt and pepper. Garnish with fresh parsley and some shavings of parmesan if desired.

VEGAN FAVORITE

GLUTEN FREE

Serves 6 | PREP TIME: 15 minutes. COOK TIME: 45 minutes.

CHAPTER TWO

SAUSAGE, BACON, BEEF, AND OTHER MEATY FLAVORS

If you like meaty soups, then you'll be happy to find a couple of favorites featured in this chapter. With varying beefy flavors, from meatball to gumbo to spicy soups, you'll be able to enjoy the fantastic flavors in these delicious dishes.

To make great meaty soups, take your time. Buy from butchers you like and trust. Meat doesn't like to be rushed, or moved around. Browning the meat properly is important to the flavor.

Heat the pot as hot as you can without the oil smoking, place the meat in carefully. It's important that you brown meat in small batches with room in the pot; too much meat will cool the pan down too fast, and the meat will release liquid and steam. So be patient and brown the meat in a few batches. Let it sizzle in the oil rather than moving it around so you get nice, flavorful, dark-brown spots.

Patience is the key to great tasting meaty soups.

SMOKED HAM WITH GREAT NORTHERN WHITE BEANS

The smoked ham hock adds a lot of flavor and body to the soup, but if you're looking for a lighter flavor, use a leaner smoked ham steak instead. This can be served with cornbread or with croutons.

Ingredients

1 lb dried Great Northern white beans

1 large red onion, chopped

1 carrot, sliced

2 stalks celery, sliced

2 tbsp butter

2 cloves garlic, minced

½ tsp salt

1 bay leaf

¼ tsp black pepper

¼ tsp thyme

64 oz chicken stock

1 smoked ham hock (about 1 lb)

Fresh parsley for garnish

Salt and pepper to taste

Note: You'll need to soak the beans overnight.

Cooking Instructions

Soak the beans in enough water to cover overnight. Add a pinch of salt to the water.

Melt the butter in a large pan over medium heat. Sauté the onion, carrot and celery in the butter until fragrant, about 5 minutes. Add the garlic, salt, bay leaf, pepper and thyme to the pot and cook for 2 minutes, stirring constantly. Add the stock, ham hock and the drained white beans to the pot and bring to a simmer. Then partly cover and cook until the beans are done, about 1 hour, stirring occasionally. Add more stock if the soup becomes too thick. Taste the soup and adjust seasonings as needed with salt and pepper. Garnish with fresh parsley and serve.

GLUTEN FREE

Serves 4 | PREP TIME: 10 minutes. COOK TIME: 1 hour 15 minutes.

BAYOU CHICKEN & SAUSAGE GUMBO

There are many variations of gumbo, and this is a version of the New Orleans tradition.

Ingredients

1 chicken, cut into 8 pieces
1 tsp paprika
1 tsp seasoned salt
½ tsp white pepper
½ cup canola oil
½ cup flour
1 large onion, diced
1 green pepper, diced
2 stalks celery, diced
1 lb Andouille sausage, cut into ½ inch chunks
5 cloves of garlic, smashed
½ tsp thyme
½ tsp salt
64 oz chicken stock
1 cup long grain white rice
1 cup frozen okra, thawed
½ tsp cayenne pepper, or to taste
1 tsp filé powder

Cooking Instructions

Mix the paprika, seasoned salt and white pepper, and sprinkle liberally over the chicken. Warm the oil in a large stockpot over medium-high heat. Brown the chicken in the hot oil, about 4 minutes per side. Remove and set aside. Lower heat to medium low and add the flour. Stir constantly with a wooden spatula to avoid burning for 15-20 minutes until a light caramel color is achieved; this is the roux that thickens the gumbo. Add the onion, pepper and celery, and cook until translucent, about 10 minutes. Add the sausage, garlic, thyme and salt, and cook for two minutes, stirring constantly. Add the reserved chicken pieces along with the chicken stock and bring the gumbo to a boil. Then turn the heat to medium low and simmer the gumbo for one hour. After an hour, remove the chicken, allow to cool and pull the meat from the bones. Add the rice directly to the pot and simmer until the rice is tender, about 20 – 25 minutes. Stir in the pulled chicken, the okra and the cayenne pepper to taste and cook for another 15 minutes to allow the flavors to develop. Remove from the heat and stir in the filé powder. Serve in deep bowls garnished with scallions.

Chef's Note:

There is 'creole' gumbo and then there's 'cajun' gumbo. Creole is the New Orleans French-Quarter style seafood gumbo, while Cajun gumbo uses more fowl and game meats, along with more peppers and heat. Filé powder is made from sassafras leaves and give gumbo its distinctive flavor. In this recipe, we cut the normal amount of okra and add only a touch of filé powder right at the end of cooking so that you can taste it but it's not overpowering.

Serves 8 | PREP TIME: 25 minutes. COOK TIME: 2 hours.

ITALIAN WEDDING SOUP

The stories behind this soup are all over the map. There's one story that though its veracity is unverified, goes as follows; this soup was served at traditional Italian weddings because the shape of the meatballs were symbolic of a well-rounded marriage for the newlyweds. It's a nice thought and a great meal to boot.

Ingredients

16 oz ground beef (we use sirloin)

2 eggs, beaten

¼ cup dried bread crumbs

¼ cup grated Parmesan cheese

½ teaspoon basil

½ teaspoon oregano

½ teaspoon thyme

1 medium onion, diced

2 medium carrots, diced

1 stalk celery, diced

1 tablespoon olive oil

2 cloves garlic, minced

32 oz chicken broth

1 bay leaf

2 cups spinach, washed, trimmed and sliced

1 cup acini de pepe pasta

Salt and pepper to taste

Cooking Instructions

Place the beef in a medium sized mixing bowl. Add the egg, bread crumbs, cheese, basil, oregano and thyme. Shape mixture into 1 inch round balls. Set meatballs aside.*

Add the olive oil to a large stockpot over medium heat. Add the onion, carrots and celery, and cook for 5 minutes. Add the garlic, chicken broth and bay leaf, and bring to a simmer. Stir in the spinach and meatballs. Allow the soup to return to a simmer; then reduce heat to medium low. Be careful not to let the soup reach a rolling boil, which could toughen the meatballs. A slow gentle poach will give you good, tender meatballs. Cook, stirring frequently, until the meatballs are no longer pink inside, about 10 minutes. Stir in the pasta and cook for an additional 5 minutes until the pasta is done.

Chef's Note:

When packing the meatballs, do it gently, and pack the meat in your hands just tightly enough to hold together when dropped into the simmering water. Try not to squeeze or knead the meat, which can make it tough.

Serves 6 | PREP TIME: 15 minutes. COOK TIME: 25 minutes.

ALBONDIGAS OR MEXICAN MEATBALL SOUP

Spicy meatballs are poached in a flavorful broth for a soup that eats like a meal.

Ingredients

1 lb ground beef (I recommend 85% lean)
1 shallot, minced
1 clove of garlic, minced
½ cup cooked rice
1 egg, beaten
½ tsp salt
½ tsp cumin
¼ tsp black pepper
2 tbsp fresh cilantro, chopped

1 medium red onion, diced
1 carrot, diced
2 stalks celery, sliced
1 tbsp canola oil
2 cloves garlic, minced
½ tsp salt
¼ tsp oregano
1 tsp chili powder
¼ tsp paprika
¼ tsp black pepper
32 oz chicken stock
3 large tomatoes, chopped
Fresh cilantro leaves for garnish

GLUTEN FREE

Cooking Instructions

Mix the beef, shallot, garlic, cooked rice, egg, salt, cumin, pepper and cilantro in a large bowl. Use a big table spoon to roll the meat mixture into balls and set them on a parchment paper-lined cookie sheet. You should have about 16-20 meatballs.

Start the soup by sautéing the onion, carrot and celery in the canola oil until fragrant, about 5 minutes. Add the garlic, salt, oregano, chili powder, paprika and pepper to the pot, and cook for 2 minutes, stirring constantly. Add the stock and the tomatoes to the pot, and bring to a simmer. Once a simmer is reached, turn the heat to low and drop the meatballs into the broth 4 or 5 at a time, then cook for 15 minutes until done. Then ladle the meatballs into individual bowls, 4 to 5 per bowl until all the meatballs are served. Taste the broth and adjust seasonings as needed with salt and pepper. Ladle the broth into the bowls and garnish with fresh cilantro.

Chef's Notes:

Like other meatball soups, be careful not to boil the meatballs or they will be tough. You're looking for a slow simmer for a gentle poach. Also, pack the meatballs lightly rather than firmly to keep them tender.

Serves 4 | PREP TIME: 15 minutes. COOK TIME: 25 minutes.

BEEF BORSCHT

A hearty and warming soup.

Ingredients

4 large beets, left whole and scrubbed well
(beet greens, sliced and reserved)

2 tbsp olive oil

Dash of salt

1 small yellow onion, diced

2 stalks of celery, sliced

2 carrots, sliced

1 tbsp butter

2 cloves garlic, minced

½ tsp salt

¼ tsp thyme

¼ tsp marjoram

¼ tsp black pepper

32 oz beef stock

1 lb bone-in beef shank

Salt and pepper to taste

Fresh dill fronds and sour cream for garnish

Cooking Instructions

Preheat oven to 350 degrees. Toss beets with 1 tablespoon of olive oil and a little salt in a large bowl. Turn out onto foil and wrap tightly. Place foil package in a pie pan and roast the beets for 1 to 1 ½ hours, or until tender. Check beets by piercing with the tip of a paring knife – finished beets will yield to the knife tip and be soft enough to slip out of their skins with a little pressure.

While the beets roast prepare the soup. Sauté the onion, celery and carrots in a large stockpot set over medium heat in the butter and the other tablespoon of olive oil until fragrant, about 8 minutes. Add the garlic, salt, thyme, marjoram and the pepper to the pot and cook for two minutes, stirring constantly. Add the stock and the beef shank and bring the soup to a simmer. Once a simmer is reached cover the pot and turn heat to low and continue cooking until the beef shank is tender, about 45 minutes to 1 hour. Remove the beef shank from the pot and set aside to cool. By now the beets should be done, so peel and quarter them before adding to the soup. Purée with an immersion blender or in your food processor in batches to a smooth consistency. Remove all bones and fat from the beef shank. Cut the meat into bite size pieces and add it and the sliced beet greens to the pot and cook for 25 minutes to allow all flavors to develop. Taste and adjust seasonings as necessary with salt and pepper as needed. Ladle into bowls and garnish with fresh dill and a dollop of sour cream.

GLUTEN
FREE

Chef's Note:

This is a very basic but very enjoyable and comforting dish, a noodle soup version of a PB&J, if you will. This is a more wholesome and tasty version of ramen, and takes about the same time to cook.

Serves 4 – 6 | PREP TIME: 15 minutes. COOK TIME: 1 to 1½ hours.

ASIAN PORK & GLASS NOODLE SOUP

Bean-thread noodles are the prime component in this flavorful and easy soup with
a touch of lemongrass and the exotic flavor of Chinese five-spice powder.
It comes together quickly and makes for a sensational lunch.

Ingredients

1 medium onion, diced

1 carrot, diced

1 stalk celery, diced

1 tbsp canola oil

2 cloves garlic, minced

½ tsp salt

1 tbsp soy sauce

½ tsp Chinese five-spice powder

1 stalk of lemongrass, crushed and cut into one-inch pieces

32 oz chicken stock

1 tbsp fish sauce

1 lb bean-thread noodles (or rice vermicelli)

1 lb pork loin, cut into thin matchsticks

Salt and pepper to taste

Fresh scallions thinly sliced for garnish

Cooking Instructions

Bring a large pot of salted water to a simmer over medium high heat. Keep hot while preparing the rest of the soup so it is ready to cook the noodles when you are.

Sauté the onion, carrot and celery in the canola oil in a large stockpot over medium heat until fragrant, about 5 minutes. Add the garlic, salt, soy sauce, Chinese five-spice powder and lemongrass to the pot and cook for 2 minutes, stirring constantly. Add the stock and fish sauce and bring to a simmer.

At this point you should drop the noodles into the hot water and finish the rest of the soup while the noodles are cooking. Follow the cooking time as indicated on the noodle packaging.

Once a simmer is reached in the soup pot, add the pork matchsticks to the hot broth and cook until just done, about 5-8 minutes. Ladle the bean-thread noodles into four bowls. Top with several ladles of the pork and broth, and garnish with fresh scallions.

Serves 4 | PREP TIME: 10 minutes. COOK TIME: 25 minutes.

VIETNAMESE PHO WITH BEEF

Pho can be made with all manner of cuts of meat and usually thin slices of beef sirloin are used in this recipe. The meat is cut very thin and then the boiling hot broth is poured over the meat and noodles once they are in the bowl, the meat on its way to your table. It's a time consuming process but all the steps are easy and the ingredients (save the culantro) are easy to find.

Ingredients

1 lbs beef-knuckle bones, with marrow

1 3-inch long cinnamon stick

4 star anise

2 tbsp brown sugar

4 whole cloves

1 lime, sliced

½ tsp salt

2 large onions, peeled and halved

1 3-inch piece of ginger, halved

2 tbsp fish sauce

2 tbsp soy sauce

2 tbsp chili paste

2 lbs beef sirloin tip, sliced thin (1/8 inch max, thinner if possible) against the grain

1 bunch of scallions, sliced

1 lb banh pho noodles (or rice vermicelli)

Fresh basil leaves, lime wedges, bean sprout, sliced jalapeño and culantro leaves for garnishes

Cooking Instructions

Put 2 quarts water in a large stockpot and set it on the stove, covered. Heat to a simmer and reserve this to cook the noodles when needed.

Place the beef bones in another large pot and cover with water. Add the cinnamon stick, star anise, brown sugar, cloves, lime and salt to the water. Bring to a boil and simmer for 1½ hours, skimming the fat that rises to the top. While that is cooking, char the onion and the ginger by holding the onion and the ginger over the open flame of your stove, using tongs. They don't have to be perfectly evenly charred on all sides, just slightly charred and semi-cooked. Add the charred onion and ginger to the beef bones in the pot and skim any fat or scum that rises to the surface. Charring adds an extra depth of flavor and is a step that should not be skipped.

Once the bones are cooked, strain the broth into another pot set over medium-high heat. Add the fish sauce, soy sauce and chili paste to the strained broth, and bring to a boil.

Cook the noodles in the heated water of the other stockpot according to package directions, and drain well.

Now its time to assemble the pho. Ladle the noodles into large deep bowls and top with several slices of raw sirloin, then cover with several ladles of the boiling hot broth. Garnish the bowls with fresh scallions and serve with other garnishes on small plates on the side.

Chef's Note:

Taking any shortcuts with this recipe just isn't worth it.

Serves 8 | PREP TIME: 30 minutes. COOK TIME: 2 hours

SPICY BEEF WITH RAMEN NOODLE SOUP

Ingredients

1 medium onion, diced

1 carrot, diced

1 stalk celery, diced

1 tbsp canola oil

1 clove of garlic, minced

½ tsp salt

1 tbsp soy sauce

1 tbsp chili paste

32 oz beef broth

1 tbsp fish sauce

1 lb ramen noodles (or rice vermicelli)

1 lb beef flank steak, cut across the grain into ⅛ inch slices

Fresh scallions, sliced for garnish

Cooking Instructions

Bring a large pot of salted water to a simmer over medium-high heat. Keep hot to cook noodles while preparing the rest of the soup.

Sauté the onion, carrot and celery in the canola oil in a large stockpot over medium heat until fragrant, about 5 minutes. Add the garlic, salt, soy sauce and chili paste, and cook for 2 minutes, stirring constantly. Add the beef broth and fish sauce, and bring to a simmer.

At this point drop the noodles into the hot water and cook the rest of the soup while the noodles are cooking.

Once a simmer is reached in the soup pot, add the flank steak to the hot broth, cooking until just done, about 5-8 minutes. Ladle the ramen noodles into four bowls. Top with several ladles of the beefy soup and garnish with fresh scallions.

Chef's Note:

This is a very basic but very enjoyable and comforting dish, a noodle soup version of a PB&J, if you will. This is a more wholesome and tasty version of ramen, and takes about the same time to cook.

Serves 4 | PREP TIME: 10 minutes. COOK TIME: 20 minutes

TACO SOUP

Ingredients

1 lb ground beef (85% lean)
1 large red onion, chopped
2 carrots, sliced
2 stalks celery, sliced
1 tbsp canola oil
2 cloves garlic, minced
½ tsp salt
¼ tsp oregano
¼ tsp paprika
¼ tsp black pepper
32 oz chicken stock
1 tsp chili powder
10 oz cooked pinto beans
Salt and pepper to taste
Fresh scallions, sour cream and shredded cheddar cheese for garnishes

GLUTEN FREE

Cooking Instructions

Brown the ground beef in a skillet over medium heat until cooked through, about 10 minutes, stirring with a wooden spatula to break up the meat into crumbles. When finished drain and set aside.

In a large stockpot over medium heat, sauté the onion, carrots and celery in the canola oil until fragrant, about 5 minutes. Add the garlic, salt, oregano, paprika and pepper to the pot and cook for 2 minutes, stirring constantly. Add the stock, ground beef, chili powder and pinto beans and bring to a simmer. Once a simmer is reached reduce heat to low and continue cooking to develop the flavors for 15 minutes. Taste the soup and adjust seasonings as needed with salt and pepper. Ladle into bowls and garnish with fresh scallions, shredded cheddar and a dollop of sour cream.

Chef's Note:

This can be served with jalapeño cheddar corn bread.
It can be garnished with tortilla chips.

Serves 4 | PREP TIME: 10 minutes. COOK TIME: 25 minutes

CHAPTER THREE

CHICKEN AND OTHER FEATHERED FRIENDS

Chicken soup is the quintessential soup dish. Most of us believe in its healing powers. In fact, science has shown that a good chicken soup has anti-inflammatory properties. Many meat eaters love their chicken soup, and pick chicken as their go-to meat when making homemade soups.

Chicken soup is versatile. There are so many different ingredients and flavor profiles that can be added to make a delectable chicken soup. It's quick, and doesn't require a lot of prep. You don't need to brown the chicken which saves time. It's an easy and accommodating flavor and goes well with many different spices.

We recommend you don't mess with your chicken stock. It's comforting. It's easy and friendly. It's chicken soup. From the classics to mouthwatering chowders, you'll learn everything you need to know about making an appetizing chicken dish.

This chapter will also feature amazing tasting soups with Turkey and Duck meats that will have you licking your spoon.

CREAMY CHICKEN & WILD RICE SOUP

An embodiment of your favorite chair or blanket, like a snuggy in a bowl.

Ingredients

1 medium onion, diced

1 medium carrot, diced

2 stalks celery, diced

½ cup butter

2 cloves garlic, minced

32 oz chicken stock

½ teaspoon thyme

½ teaspoon sage

1 cup uncooked wild rice

3 cups milk, more as needed

¼ cup all purpose flour

2 cups cooked, cubed chicken breast or thigh

Salt and pepper to taste

Cooking Instructions

In a large stockpot, sweat the onion, celery and carrot in the butter over medium heat until translucent, about 10 minutes. Add the garlic and cook two minutes longer. Add the chicken stock, thyme and sage along with the wild rice. Bring to a simmer and cook for 25 minutes with the lid on. Remove lid and check the doneness of the wild rice; if it's tender, proceed, if not, cover and cook for another ten minutes.

In the meantime whisk the milk and flour together. Once the wild rice is tender add the milk and flour mixture to the soup along with the cooked chicken. Bring up to a simmer for 15-20 minutes and allow the soup to thicken. Add salt and pepper to taste. Add more milk if the soup gets too thick.

Serves 6 | PREP TIME: 15 minutes. COOK TIME: 45 minutes.

ROSEMARY CHICKEN DUMPLING SOUP

This recipe is low in sodium and fat. It is filled with herbs to boost the flavor, rosemary in particular and dumplings to make it special.

Ingredients

1 medium onion, diced
2 stalks celery, diced
1 medium carrot, diced
2 tbsp olive oil
2 cloves garlic, minced
32 oz chicken stock
2 cups cooked chicken, shredded
½ tsp thyme
1 tsp rosemary
2 bay leaves
Salt and pepper to taste

DUMPLINGS

1 ½ cups all-purpose flour
½ tsp salt
½ tsp baking powder
3 tbsp butter
1 egg, beaten
½ cup whole milk
Cold water as needed

Cooking Instructions

In a large stockpot, sweat the onion, celery, and carrot in the olive oil over medium heat for 10 minutes. Add the garlic and cook two minutes longer. Add the chicken stock, chicken and dried herbs. Bring the soup to a simmer and cook for 15 minutes with the lid on.

While the soup simmers, make the dumplings. Combine the flour, salt and baking powder in a mixing bowl. Mix in the butter and stir until well incorporated. Add egg and milk, and mix thoroughly. Mixture should be slightly wet; add cold water as needed to make the dough pliable. When the dough is finished drop spoonfuls into the warm (but not boiling) soup. The dumplings will cook in about ten minutes. Be careful to keep the soup under a boil or the dumplings will toughen. Add salt and pepper to taste and serve.

Serves 8 | PREP TIME: 25 minutes. COOK TIME: 40 minutes.

ROASTED CHICKEN FLORENTINE

The spinach and parmesan tortellini finished with a touch of whole milk make this a good, hearty soup and the perfect meal for a fall day.

Ingredients

1 medium onion, diced

2 stalks of celery, diced

1 carrot, diced

2 tbsp olive oil

1 tbsp flour

2 cloves of garlic, minced

½ tsp salt

¼ tsp thyme

¼ tsp black pepper

32 oz chicken stock

1 cup whole milk

2 cups fresh spinach, washed and trimmed

1 lb pre-roasted chicken, cubed

1 lb spinach and parmesan tortellini

fresh parsley for garnish

Cooking Instructions

Sauté the onion, celery and carrot in the olive oil in a large stockpot set over medium heat until translucent, about 8 minutes. Add the flour, garlic, salt, thyme and pepper, and cook for 2 minutes, stirring constantly. Add the stock and milk, and bring to a boil. Then add the spinach, cubed chicken and tortellini, and cook until done, about 10 minutes. Taste and adjust seasonings as necessary with salt and pepper. Garnish with fresh parsley and serve with toasted garlic bread.

Chef's Note:

You can make this with a stew-like texture by adding two tablespoons of flour instead of one.

Serves 4 | PREP TIME: 10 minutes. COOK TIME: 20 minutes.

TORTELLINI CON BRODO

Translated simply as 'tortellini in broth,' this wonderfully easy-to-make soup is very satisfying and comes together in minutes. Benissimo!

Ingredients

1 shallot, minced

1 stalk of celery, diced

1 carrot, diced

2 tsp olive oil

1 clove of garlic, minced

½ tsp salt

¼ tsp black pepper

48 oz chicken stock

1 lb of your favorite prepackaged tortellini (we use roasted chicken & ricotta)

Salt and pepper to taste

Fresh parsley, chopped for garnish

Cooking Instructions

Sauté the shallot, celery and carrot in the olive oil in a large stockpot set over medium heat until translucent, about 8 minutes. Add the garlic, salt and pepper to the pot and cook for two minutes, stirring constantly. Add the stock to the pot and bring to a boil. Once the soup reaches a boil, add the tortellini and cook per the package instructions. Taste and adjust seasonings as necessary with salt and pepper. Garnish with fresh parsley and serve.

Chef's Note:

This dish is simple and easy, yet still retains a homemade feel and flavor.

Serves 4 | PREP TIME: 10 minutes. COOK TIME: 20 minutes.

SICILIAN CHICKEN SOUP WITH BOWTIE PASTA

This is a soul satisfying chicken noodle soup.
It makes a great lunch served with a salad and some fresh breadsticks.

Ingredients

1 small yellow onion, diced
2 stalks of celery, diced (leaves included)
1 carrot, diced
2 tsp olive oil
2 cloves garlic, minced
½ tsp salt
¼ tsp basil
¼ tsp oregano
¼ tsp rosemary
¼ tsp black pepper
1 tbsp tomato paste
48 oz chicken stock
1 cup bowtie pasta
1 lb cooked chicken, cubed
2 tbsp flat-leaf Italian parsley, minced
Salt and pepper to taste
Fresh parsley, chopped for garnish

Cooking Instructions

Sauté the onion, celery and carrot in the olive oil in a large stockpot set over medium heat until translucent, about 8 minutes. Add the garlic, salt, basil, oregano, rosemary, pepper and tomato paste, and cook for two minutes, stirring constantly. Add the stock to the pot and bring to a boil. Then add the pasta and cook per the package instructions until al dente, about 8 minutes. When the pasta is done, stir in the chicken and parsley, and warm through, about 5 minutes longer. Taste and adjust seasonings as necessary with salt and pepper. Garnish with more fresh parsley.

Chef's Note:

A nice spin on the classic chicken noodle soup.

Serves 4-6 | PREP TIME: 10 minutes. COOK TIME: 25 minutes.

SPICY MAYAN CHICKEN ENCHILADA

The chipotle in this recipe adds a little heat,
and the queso fresco adds a smooth finish.

Ingredients

1 large onion, diced

2 carrots, diced

2 stalks celery, diced

1 tbsp canola oil

2 cloves garlic, minced

2 tsp ground cumin

2 tbsp chili powder

4 cups chopped fresh tomatoes or
2 (14.5 ounce) cans diced tomatoes

2 cups tomato sauce

1 chopped chipotle pepper

32 oz chicken stock

1 cup cooked black beans

1 cup corn kernels, fresh or frozen

2 cups cooked chicken, shredded

Salt and pepper to taste

4 oz crumbled queso fresco

Cooking Instructions

Warm the oil in a stockpot over medium heat. Add the onion, carrot and celery, and sauté until softened, about 10 minutes. Add the garlic and dry spices, and cook until fragrant, about one minute. Add the tomatoes, chipotle pepper and chicken stock. Bring to a simmer and cook for 15 minutes. Add the beans, corn and chicken. Return to a simmer and cook another 15 minutes to allow the flavors to develop. Taste and add salt or pepper as needed. Right before service, add the queso fresco and stir to combine.

Serves 8 | PREP TIME: 15 minutes. COOK TIME: 45 minutes.

CHICKEN AZTECA

The depth of flavor in this soup comes from dried pasilla and ancho chiles combined with a hint of lime. Almost stew-like; this recipe is equally at home as a lunch on a blustery day or as the main attraction at your Super Bowl party.

Ingredients

1 large red onion, diced

2 stalks of celery, diced

2 carrots, sliced

1 tbsp olive oil

3 cloves garlic, minced

½ tsp salt

½ tsp cumin

¼ tsp paprika

½ tsp oregano

¼ tsp epazote

¼ tsp chili powder

¼ tsp black pepper

4 dried pasilla peppers, rehydrated, seeded and chopped

4 dried ancho peppers, rehydrated, seeded and chopped

32 oz chicken stock

4 medium tomatoes, peeled, seeded and chopped

1 cup long grain white rice

1 lb roasted chicken, shredded

2 tbsp lime juice

Salt and pepper to taste

Fresh scallions and sour cream for garnish

Cooking Instructions

Sauté the onion, celery and carrots in a large stockpot set over medium heat in the olive oil until the onions are translucent, about 8 minutes. Add the garlic, salt, cumin, paprika, oregano, epazote, chili powder and pepper along with the pasilla and ancho peppers to the pot, and cook for two minutes, stirring constantly. Add the stock and tomatoes, and bring to a simmer. Once the soup reaches a simmer, add the rice, cover the pot and turn heat to low. Continue cooking until the rice is done, about 15-20 minutes. Then add the lime juice and shredded chicken, and warm through, about 3 minutes more. Taste and adjust seasonings as necessary with salt and pepper. Ladle soup into bowls and garnish with fresh scallions and a dollop of sour cream.

Chef's Note:
This recipe is filled with interesting and complex flavors.
Works in a slow cooker, too.

Serves 4-6 | PREP TIME: 20 minutes. COOK TIME: 1 hour.

MEXICAN TORTILLA SOUP

This dish has a nice medium body, a classic tomato and
chicken-broth base, and great Latin spices to give it some south-of-the-border pizazz.

Ingredients

1 large onion diced

1 stalk celery diced

1 carrot diced

2 tablespoons canola oil

2 cloves garlic, minced

4 cups fresh tomatoes, rough dice or
2 (14.5 ounce) cans diced tomatoes

32 oz chicken stock

1 chipotle pepper and 1 teaspoon of the
adobo sauce they come packed in

1 teaspoon ground cumin

1 tablespoon ancho chile powder

1 cup cooked black beans

1 cup corn kernels, fresh or frozen

16 oz cooked chicken breast, ½ inch dice

Salt and pepper to taste

¼ cup chopped fresh cilantro

Juice from 2 limes

Cooking Instructions

Warm the canola oil in a stockpot over medium heat. Add the onion, carrot and celery, and sauté until just softened, about 5 minutes. Add the garlic, tomatoes, chicken stock and chipotle along with the cumin and chili powders. Bring the soup to a simmer and cook for 20 minutes. Add the beans, corn and chicken. Return to a simmer and cook for another 15 minutes to allow the flavors to develop. Taste and add salt or pepper as needed. Right before service, stir in the cilantro and lime juice.

Serves 6 | PREP TIME: 20 minutes. COOK TIME: 30 minutes.

CARIBBEAN JERK CHICKEN CHOWDER

This dish can be served with corn muffins.

Ingredients

2 shallots, diced

2 stalks of celery, diced (leaves included)

2 carrots, sliced

1 tbsp olive oil

2 cloves garlic, minced

½ tsp salt

¼ tsp allspice

½ tsp thyme

¼ tsp pepper

32 oz chicken stock

Juice from 1 orange

Juice from 2 limes

1 tbsp cider vinegar

1 habanero pepper, seeds removed and diced

2 bone-in chicken breasts

2 bone-in chicken thighs

2 medium potatoes, peeled and cut into ½ inch chunks

1 tbsp honey, or to taste

2 ears of sweet corn, kernels cut from the cob

Salt and pepper to taste

Fresh parsley

Cooking Instructions

Sauté the shallots, celery and carrots in the olive oil in a large stockpot set over medium heat for 8 minutes. Add the garlic, salt, allspice, thyme and pepper, and cook for two minutes, stirring constantly. Add the stock, orange juice, lime juice, cider vinegar and habanero pepper, and bring to a simmer. Then add the chicken and cook for 30 minutes. Add the potatoes and cook until tender, about 15 minutes longer. Turn the heat to low, check to make sure the chicken is cooked through and remove to a plate. Add the honey to the chowder. Taste and adjust seasonings as necessary with salt and pepper or more honey. Take the meat off the bones and shred the chicken. Add the corn and shredded chicken to the chowder and warm through. Taste one final time to adjust seasonings if necessary. Garnish with fresh parsley.

Chef's Note:

This is a great departure from traditional creamy corn chowders.

Serves 4-6 | PREP TIME: 10 minutes. COOK TIME: 1 hour.

ROASTED TURKEY WITH EGG NOODLE SOUP

This soup is too good to make only once a year when you're trying to figure out what to do with leftover turkey! You can serve this with corn muffins and honey butter.

Ingredients

1 large Vidalia onion, diced

2 stalks of celery, diced

2 carrots, sliced

2 cloves garlic, minced

1 tbsp olive oil

½ tsp salt

¼ tsp thyme

¼ tsp marjoram

¼ tsp ground sage

¼ tsp black pepper

1 whole smoked turkey leg

48 oz chicken stock

1 16 oz package uncooked egg noodles

Salt and pepper to taste

Fresh parsley for garnish

Note: You may need to go to your local butcher to find or order a smoked turkey leg, especially off season.

Cooking Instructions

Sauté the onion, celery and carrots in the olive oil in a large stockpot set over medium heat until the onions are translucent, about 8 minutes. Add the garlic, salt, thyme, marjoram, sage and pepper, and cook for two minutes, stirring constantly. Add the turkey leg and stock, and bring to a simmer. Then cover the pot, turn the heat to low and continue cooking to allow the flavors to develop for 30 minutes. Remove the turkey leg with tongs and set aside to cool. Raise the heat and bring the soup to a boil. Add the egg noodles and cook per the package instructions, about 10 minutes. Shred the meat from the turkey leg while the noodles are cooking. Once the noodles are done, return the turkey meat to the pot and warm through, about 5 minutes more. Taste and adjust seasonings as necessary with salt and pepper. Ladle soup into bowls and garnish with fresh parsley.

Chef's Note:

This is another simple recipe proving that fifteen steps aren't necessary to get dinner on the table. The cooking time can be cut further if you shred the turkey-leg meat and don't cook it with the broth, but you'll sacrifice some flavor.

Serves 4–6 | PREP TIME: 10 minutes. COOK TIME: 45 minutes.

GREEK AVGOLEMONO SOUP

This wonderful broth-based soup is thickened with egg, has a great lemony zest to it and has been around for literally centuries for good reason.

Ingredients

1 shallot, minced

1 clove of garlic, minced

1 tbsp olive oil

48 oz chicken stock

½ tsp salt

¼ tsp white pepper

½ cup orzo or rice

2 eggs

Juice from 2 lemons

1 lb cooked boneless skinless chicken breast, shredded

Salt and pepper to taste

Fresh parsley and lemon wedge for garnish

Cooking Instructions

Sauté the shallot and garlic in the olive oil in a large stockpot set over medium heat for 2 minutes. Add the stock, salt and pepper, and bring to a boil. Once the soup is boiling, add the orzo and cook until done, about 7-10 minutes. Turn the heat to low. Crack the eggs into a large bowl and whisk until frothy, about 3-5 minutes. Add the lemon juice to the eggs and whisk until fully incorporated. Whisk a little of the hot broth, ½ cup at a time, into the egg and lemon-juice mixture until the mix is tempered, about 1.5 cups of broth total. Be sure to mix thoroughly after each time you add broth to keep the eggs from scrambling. Once the broth is whisked in and the eggs are tempered, add the egg mixture back to the pot and stir well. Do not allow the soup to reach a boil or the eggs will scramble. Add the shredded chicken and warm through. Taste the soup and adjust seasonings as necessary with salt and pepper. Garnish with fresh parsley and serve with wedges of lemon.

Chef's Note:

This soup is fairly simple. Done well this can become one of your favorite soups with the acid of the lemon balanced by the salty richness from the broth.

Serves 4-6 | PREP TIME: 10 minutes. COOK TIME: 20 minutes.

CHAPTER FOUR

CREAMY, CHEESY OR TOMATO-Y SOUPS, AND BISQUES

These soups are comfort in a spoon. Many go for the cream of broccoli because it's comforting, and being comfortable helps a person heal.

A bisque uses heat to transform small pieces of traditionally leftover food into something amazing that captures the essence of the flavor in a distinctive, elegant, and smooth meal.

A couple of practical notes for this chapter: When a soup recipe calls for cheese, be careful not to add it all at once. Stir it well while it's being added so it doesn't become stringy in the soup. Also make sure you add the cheese, or cream for that matter, off the heat. If either is subjected to too high a temperature, it will break which means the the fat will separate, and you will get oily spots on the top and the rest at the bottom.

These soups are some of the most popular. They're the richest, and fill you up while warming your bones.

LOBSTER BISQUE

This dish is very rich and decadent. It doesn't use large chunks of lobster;
just the essence of lobster in the tradition of a true bisque.

Ingredients

1 medium onion, diced

1 medium carrot, diced

2 stalks celery, diced

1 clove of garlic, minced

4 tbsp butter, divided

2 bay leaves

½ tsp dried thyme

1 cup white wine

1 whole 2 lb lobster, cooked and shelled,
claw and tail meat removed and cut into small
dice (reserve the rest of the lobster including
the shell)

32 oz chicken stock

2 tbsp flour

2 tbsp tomato paste

1 cup heavy cream

¼ cup sherry

Salt and pepper to taste

Cooking Instructions

In a large pan, sauté the onion, carrot, celery and garlic in 2 tablespoons of butter over medium-high heat. Sweat the aromatics until translucent, about 6-8 minutes. Add the bay leaves and thyme, and stir for 1 minute. Deglaze the pan with the wine, then add the reserved lobster and shells, and cook for another 5 minutes. Add half the chicken stock and bring to a boil. Allow the soup to reduce for 5 minutes. Turn off the heat and transfer the entire batch to a stockpot; pouring the soup through a fine-mesh strainer, and pushing down with a spatula to insure you extract every last bit of flavorful stock. Melt the rest of the butter in a small saucepan on medium heat and add the flour, stirring constantly for 5 minutes until brown and incorporated. (You're making a roux to thicken the bisque.) While the roux is cooking add the tomato paste and the rest of the chicken stock to the bisque in the stockpot over medium heat. Add the finished roux to the bisque all at once and stir thoroughly. Allow the soup to come to a simmer. The soup will thicken as it cooks. Then remove it from the heat and add the cream, sherry and reserved lobster meat. Taste and adjust seasonings as needed with salt and pepper.

Serves 8 | PREP TIME: 15 minutes. COOK TIME: 35 minutes.

BROCCOLI & WHITE CHEDDAR SOUP

Ingredients

1 medium onion, diced

1 medium carrot, diced

2 heads broccoli, cut into florets with stems peeled and cut into a small dice

4 tbsp butter

2 cloves garlic, minced

½ tsp thyme

¼ tsp marjoram

½ tsp salt

4 tbsp all-purpose flour

32 oz vegetable stock

16 oz whole milk

3 cups grated white cheddar cheese

Salt and pepper to taste

Cooking Instructions

In a large stockpot with a lid, sweat the onion, carrot and diced broccoli stems in 2 tablespoons of the butter over medium heat until translucent, about 10 minutes. Add the garlic and cook 2 minutes longer. Add the dried herbs, the rest of the butter and all of the flour, and stir well. Cook for 3-5 minutes until the flour is well incorporated, stirring constantly. Add the chicken stock and milk, and bring to a simmer. Add the broccoli florets and allow the soup to cook at a simmer for 20 minutes; it will thicken as it cooks. Then remove the soup from the heat and add the cheese, one cup at a time, stirring constantly to make sure it melts smoothly. Then taste the soup and adjust with salt and pepper as needed. Thin with a little more milk if desired.

Chef's Note:

You need to stir this soup like a madman when you first add the flour and when the cheese hits the flour later. Otherwise it will burn, and you will have to start the process over.

Serves 8 | PREP TIME: 20 minutes. COOK TIME: 40-45 minutes.

CHICKPEA CHOWDER WITH PURSLANE & LEEKS

Purslane is a wild green that became popular in the food industry years ago.
It has a sharp, bitter green flavor like a peppery augula
that gives the soup a good zippy flavor.

Ingredients

2 leeks, root and tops removed, sliced
1 medium carrot, diced
2 stalks celery, diced
2 tbsp olive oil
2 cloves garlic, minced
1 tsp thyme
2 bay leaves
32 oz vegetable stock
1 tsp salt
1 pinch red pepper flakes
2 cups chickpeas, soaked overnight
1 large potato, medium dice
1 bunch purslane, chopped *
Salt and pepper to taste

Note: You'll need to soak the chickpeas overnight.

Cooking Instructions

Sauté the leeks, carrot, and celery in the oil in a stockpot over medium heat until translucent; about 10 minutes. Add the garlic and dried herbs, and cook for one minute. Add the vegetable stock, salt and red pepper flakes, and bring to a simmer, stirring occasionally. When the soup has reached a simmer, add the chickpeas and potato, and cook until tender, approximately 25-30 minutes. Once the potato and the chickpeas are tender, add the purslane and cook for 5 minutes longer. Taste the soup and adjust seasonings with salt and pepper as needed.

Chef's Note:

You can substitute one bunch of spinach or kale for the purslane if it's not available.

Serves 6 | PREP TIME: 10 minutes. COOK TIME: 45 minutes.

BEER & CHEESE WITH SMOKED BACON SOUP

Ingredients

1 medium onion, diced

2 stalks celery, diced

1 medium carrot, diced

2 tbsp olive oil

2 cloves garlic, minced

12 oz beer, any medium-body brew will work

24 oz chicken stock

8 oz cooked smoked bacon, chopped

4 tbsp butter

4 tbsp all-purpose flour

24 oz whole milk

5 cups grated cheddar cheese

1 tbsp spicy mustard

2 tsp hot sauce

Salt and pepper to taste

Cooking Instructions

In a large stockpot with a lid, sweat the onion, celery, and carrot in the butter over medium heat until translucent, about 10 minutes. Add the garlic and cook two minutes longer. Add the beer and stir well, then add the chicken stock and bacon. Bring to a simmer and cook for 15 minutes and remove from heat.

While the vegetables and beer are cooking, make the cheese base in another large pot with a heavy bottom. Melt the butter over medium heat and add the flour all at once. Stir constantly as the flour cooks and starts to darken slightly. Stir in the milk a cup at a time and keep the mixture moving to avoid scorching the roux, for about a minute or two. The mixture will thicken as it heats. Once the last cup of milk is incorporated remove the mixture from the heat and stir in the grated cheese one cup at a time until incorporated.

Over low heat, mix the vegetables and beer into the cheese base one cup at a time, making sure to stir thoroughly after each addition. Add mustard and hot sauce. Taste and adjust seasoning with salt and pepper as desired.

Serves 8 | PREP TIME: 20 minutes. COOK TIME: 40 minutes.

THE DIVINE CREAM OF MUSHROOM SOUP

This is a decadent soup for lunch as well as a wonderful treat as a first course in a special meal.

Ingredients

16 oz button mushrooms, sliced
1 tsp salt
2 tbsp olive oil
4 medium shallots, thinly sliced
3 cloves garlic, minced
2 tbsp butter
5 tbsp flour
6 cups chicken stock
2 tsp thyme
2 tsp parsley
½ cup heavy cream
Salt and pepper to taste

Cooking Instructions

Heat the olive oil in a large pot over medium-high heat. Add the mushrooms and a tsp of salt, and cook, stirring occasionally until soft, about 6 minutes. Add the shallots and cook, stirring occasionally, another 3 minutes. Add the garlic and cook for another 3 minutes. Stir in the butter. Add the flour and cook, stirring constantly, for 2 minutes more. Pour in the broth, and bring to a boil while stirring. Add the thyme and parsley, and lower the heat to medium low. Simmer for 10 minutes. Whisk the heavy cream into the soup and season with salt and pepper to taste.

Chef's Note:

People don't eat mushrooms often enough and then don't cook them long enough. You want to cook them to get the water out so the concentrated flavors can mingle nicely with the other spices and sauces in the dish. Don't skimp on the six-minute sauté time, it's worth it.

Serves 6 | PREP TIME: 15 minutes. COOK TIME: 25 Minutes.

CHIPOTLE SWEET-POTATO BISQUE

Warm and comforting, this easy bisque gets a flavor charge from spicy and savory canned chipotle chiles. The chipotles lend a smoky and spicy counterpoint to the earthy sweet potatoes. This can be garnished with a bit of sour cream and fresh parsley.

Ingredients

2 large carrots, diced

3 shallots, diced

2 stalks celery, diced

2 tbsp olive oil

2 cloves garlic, minced

1 canned chipotle, chopped, plus 1 tsp of the adobo sauce they are packed in

½ tsp oregano

½ tsp salt

¼ tsp freshly ground black pepper

32 oz vegetable stock

2 large sweet potatoes, peeled and quartered

2 Yukon Gold potatoes, peeled and quartered

Salt and pepper to taste

Cooking Instructions

Sauté the carrot, shallot and celery in a large stockpot set over medium heat until fragrant, about 5 minutes. Add the garlic, chipotle, oregano, salt and pepper, and cook for one minute, stirring constantly. Add the stock and bring the soup to a simmer. Then add the potatoes and cook until the potatoes are tender, about 30 minutes. Pulse with an immersion blender or blend in batches in your food processor until smooth. Taste the soup and adjust seasonings as necessary with salt and pepper.

Chef's Note:

If you'd like it a bit spicier, add another chipotle.

VEGAN FAVORITE

GLUTEN FREE

Serves 4-6 | PREP TIME: 10 minutes. COOK TIME: 45 minutes.

CREAM OF POTATO & LEEK SOUP

This is a classic flavor combination inspired by the cold French soup vichyssoise.

Ingredients

1 leek, chopped, including the green part

1 stalk celery, chopped

1 carrot, shredded

2 cloves garlic, minced

4 tbsp of butter

¼ cup all-purpose flour

2 cups chicken stock

3 potatoes cut in ¼ inch cubes

2 cups milk

1 tablespoon chopped fresh parsley

¼ teaspoon thyme

¼ teaspoon rosemary

Dash of hot sauce (like Tabasco sauce)

Dash of Worcestershire sauce

Salt and pepper to taste

Cooking Instructions

In a large stockpot, sweat the leek, celery, carrot, and garlic in the butter over medium heat, until just softened. Add the flour and stir constantly for 2 or 3 minutes. Add the chicken stock into the pot slowly, stirring as you add. Add the potatoes, milk, parsley, thyme, rosemary, hot sauce, and Worcestershire. Simmer for 20 to 30 minutes, stirring frequently, until the potatoes are soft.

Serves 6 | PREP TIME: 20 minutes. COOK TIME: 35 minutes.

ROASTED TOMATO & RED PEPPER BISQUE

Roasting vegetables is a quick and simple way to bring out their inherent natural sweetness as in the simple recipe. To Garnish, you can add a dollop of sour cream or plain yogurt to set off the color and add a bit of creaminess.

Ingredients

2 lbs fresh Roma or other plum tomatoes, cut in half and seeded

3 large red peppers, cut in half and seeded

1 medium onion, quartered

1 medium carrot, quartered

½ tsp salt

2 tbsp olive oil

2 bay leaves

¼ tsp thyme

¼ tsp oregano

¼ tsp basil

32 oz chicken stock

Salt and pepper to taste

GLUTEN FREE

Cooking Instructions

Heat oven to 425 degrees. Toss the tomatoes, peppers, onions and carrots in the salt and olive oil them turn out onto a foil-lined baking sheet. Roast the vegetables in the oven until softened, about 25 minutes. Remove the roasted vegetables, place in a large bowl and cover tightly for 10 minutes. Once the vegetables have cooled enough to touch, remove the skins from the peppers and put everything into a large stockpot set over medium heat. Add the dried herbs and chicken stock, and bring to a simmer. Then cook for an additional 15 minutes, stirring occasionally. Remove the soup from the heat, take the bay leaves out, and purée with an immersion blender or your food processor in batches to a smooth consistency. Taste the soup and adjust seasonings with salt and pepper as needed.

Chef's Note:

You may need to pass this soup through a strainer to get all the bits of tomato and pepper skins out for an extra smooth consistency.

Serves 6 | PREP TIME: 10 COOK TIME: 50 minutes.

CHAPTER FIVE

FANTASTIC FISH, SEAFOOD, AND OTHER HEARTY CHOWDERS

Fish and shellfish soups offer different tastes and textures than other soups in this book. The sea makes them distinctive, sometimes higher end but always new and different. Fish flavors are relatively mild, so generally, you don't want to use aggressive spices. You don't want to overwhelm the flavors to keep the fish nice, light, and delicate.

It's good to remember for this chapter that fish cooks quickly in soups. Be careful to not overcook it or it will be rubbery. Perfectly cooked fish is flaky and wonderful. Quality seafood makes a huge difference in the flavor. Spending your money when buying fish will be worth it.

Like meat, fish also has a variety of options to choose from, and if you're a fish lover, you'll find some of these soups comforting too. Some of the highlights of this chapter include clam, shrimp, crab, shellfish, and oyster. You'll savor an assortment of flavorful fishes and probably have some favorites that you will be able to share with loved ones for years to come.

CIOPPINO SOUP

This is a take on Cioppino, a San Francisco classic, featuring the bounty of the sea swimming in tasty tomato-based broth. You can serve this in freshly baked sourdough-bread bowls like they do in San Francisco.

Ingredients

1 large red onion, diced

2 carrots, diced

2 stalks celery, diced

2 tbsp olive oil

2 tbsp butter

4 cloves garlic, minced

½ tsp salt

¼ tsp black pepper

¼ tsp paprika

½ tsp thyme

2 bay leaves

3 tbsp tomato paste

1 cup dry white wine

48 oz fish stock (chicken stock can be substituted)

3 tbsp cornstarch mixed with 3 tbsp cold water

1 lb firm white fish such as halibut, cut into 1-inch pieces

1 lb fresh clams, scrubbed and soaked for 20 minutes in fresh cold water to get the grit out

1 lb fresh mussels, scrubbed, debearded and soaked for 20 minutes in fresh cold water to get the grit out

2 lbs jumbo raw shrimp, shelled and cleaned

Salt and pepper to taste

Note: Don't forget to soak the mussels and clams in cold water for 20 minutes to get the grit out.

Cooking Instructions

Melt the butter with the olive oil over medium heat in a large stockpot. Sauté the onions, carrot and celery in the butter and oil until fragrant, about 5 minutes. Add the garlic, salt, pepper, paprika, thyme, bay leaves and tomato paste, and cook for 2 minutes, stirring constantly. Deglaze the pan with the white wine and reduce by half. Then add the stock and bring to a simmer. Cook until the flavors develop, about 15 minutes. Thicken the soup with the cornstarch slurry and cook until the starch taste disappears, about 5 minutes longer. Add the fish filets and cook until just done, about 5 minutes. Add the clams and mussels and cook until they open, about 5-7 minutes longer. Finally add the shrimp and cook until pink and curled, about 5 minutes. Taste the cioppino and adjust seasonings as necessary with salt and pepper.

Chef's Note:

This is an expensive dish but worth it, and entirely easier and lighter than a bouillabaisse. It is hard to imagine that this big-ticket recipe originated from a puréed vegetable soup with the addition of trimmings from a fishmonger.

GLUTEN FREE

Serves 6 | PREP TIME: 15 minutes. COOK TIME: 30 minutes.

NANTUCKET OYSTER STEW

The northeast coast of America has long been home to some of the finest oyster beds in the world, and this simple and tasty stew is an example of the many ways to eat them.

Ingredients

2 shallots, diced

1 carrot, diced

2 stalks celery, diced

2 tbsp canola oil

2 tbsp butter

2 cloves garlic, minced

½ tsp salt

¼ tsp white pepper

¼ tsp paprika

2 tbsp flour

16 oz fish stock

16 oz whole milk

2 medium potatoes, peeled and diced

1 lb freshly shucked oysters, with their liquor (about 35-40 oysters)

¼ cup heavy cream

Salt and pepper to taste

GLUTEN FREE

Cooking Instructions

Sauté the shallots, carrots and the celery in the canola oil and butter in a large stockpot set over medium heat until fragrant, about 5 minutes. Add the garlic, salt, pepper, paprika and flour, and cook for 5 minutes, stirring constantly. Add the stock and milk, and bring to a simmer. Add the potatoes and cook for 15 minutes. The soup will thicken as the potatoes cook. Add the oysters and their liquor, cook until the edges curl and they are just done, about 5 minutes. Remove from the heat and stir in the cream. Adjust seasonings as necessary with salt and pepper.

Chef's Note:

You can use Wellfleet oysters for this recipe. They tend to have deep cups which allow one to preserve as much of the oyster liquor as possible when shucking. Canned oysters can be substituted, but aren't as flavorful for this stew.

Serves 4 | PREP TIME: 10 minutes. COOK TIME: 35 minutes.

NEW ENGLAND CLAM CHOWDER

This is a take on a regional classic favorite. Clam chowder is just great, so why mess with it.
Use high-quality seafood; it makes a big difference.

Ingredients

5 lbs fresh sea clams or 2 lbs clam meat, chopped. Allow the clams to sit in fresh water for 20 minutes to get the sand out

1 medium onion, diced

2 stalks celery, diced

4 oz salt pork, medium diced

1 clove garlic, minced

1 sprig fresh thyme

1 bay leaf

¼ cup white wine

24 oz clam broth (chicken or fish stock can be substituted)

3 medium potatoes, diced

1 tbsp cornstarch mixed with 2 tbsp water

1 cup heavy cream

Salt and pepper to taste

Note: Don't forget to soak the mussels and clams in cold water for 20 minutes to get the grit out.

Cooking Instructions

Steam fresh clams until just opened, about 4 minutes. Shuck the clams and then chop and set aside. Be careful to reserve any liquid from the clams (note: if using precooked or canned clams skip to next step). Sauté the salt pork in a large stockpot over medium heat for 5 minutes. Add the onion, celery and garlic, and cook for another 8 minutes until translucent. Add the fresh thyme and bay leaf, and cook for another 5 minutes. Deglaze the pan with white wine and reduce the liquid for 3 minutes. Add the clam broth and bring the chowder to a simmer. Add the potatoes and cook for another 15 minutes until they are fork tender. Add the cornstarch and allow the chowder to thicken, about 5 minutes. Remove from heat. Remove the thyme and the bay leaf, and add the clams and heavy cream. Taste and adjust seasonings with salt and pepper as needed.

Serves 4 | PREP TIME: 15 minutes. COOK TIME: 30 minutes.

MARYLAND CRAB CHOWDER

This simple East Coast classic comes together quickly and is lighter than most chowders in a nice way. Some crusty sourdough bread and a cold beer make this a perfect dinner.

Ingredients

2 shallots, diced

2 stalks celery, diced

2 tbsp canola oil

2 cloves garlic, minced

½ tsp salt

¼ tsp white pepper

¼ tsp paprika

¼ tsp red chili flakes

16 oz fish stock

16 oz whole milk

2 medium potatoes, peeled and diced

1 lb lump crab meat, picked over to remove shells

1 cup corn kernels, fresh or frozen

½ cup English peas, fresh or frozen

1 tbsp cornstarch mixed with 1 tbsp cold milk

Salt and pepper to taste

GLUTEN FREE

Cooking Instructions

Sauté the shallots and celery in the canola oil in a large stockpot set over medium heat until fragrant, about 5 minutes. Add the garlic, salt, pepper, paprika and chili flakes, and cook for 2 minutes, stirring constantly. Add the stock and milk, and bring to a simmer. Then add the potatoes and cook for 15 minutes until tender. Add the crab meat, corn and peas, and cook until warmed through, about 5 minutes. Thicken the chowder with the cornstarch slurry, being sure to cook the starch taste out, 5 more minutes. Adjust seasonings as necessary with salt and pepper.

Chef's Note:

This is one of the best uses for leftover crab meat, besides maybe crab cakes.

Serves 4 | PREP TIME: 10 minutes. COOK TIME: 35 minutes.

ALASKAN KING CRAB & SWEET CORN CHOWDER

The sweetness of the crab and corn is nicely balanced with potatoes and paprika, then smoothed with a bit of cream, a winning combination.

Ingredients

2 shallots, diced

2 stalks celery, diced

1 carrot, diced

1 tbsp olive oil

2 cloves garlic, minced

½ tsp Old Bay Seasoning

¼ tsp salt

¼ tsp black pepper

¼ tsp paprika

¼ tsp thyme

2 bay leaves

1 cup dry white wine

24 oz fish stock (chicken stock can be substituted)

3 medium Yukon gold potatoes, diced

2 tbsp cornstarch mixed with 2 tbsp cold milk

1 ½ lbs Alaskan king crab meat, shelled and cleaned

1 cup sweet corn kernels, fresh or frozen

8 oz heavy cream

Salt and pepper to taste

Fresh parsley, chopped for garnish

Cooking Instructions

Sauté the shallots, carrot and celery in the oil in a large stockpot set over medium heat until fragrant, about 5 minutes. Add the garlic, Old Bay Seasoning, salt, pepper, paprika, thyme and bay leaves, and cook for 2 minutes, stirring constantly. Deglaze the pan with the white wine and reduce by half. Add the stock and bring to a simmer. Add the potatoes and cook until tender, about 15 minutes. Thicken with the cornstarch slurry and cook until the starch taste disappears, about 5 minutes longer. Add the crab meat and corn. Cook until warmed through, about 5 minutes. Stir in the heavy cream and remove immediately from heat. Taste and adjust seasonings as necessary with salt and pepper. Garnish with fresh parsley.

GLUTEN FREE

Serves 6 | PREP TIME: 15 minutes. COOK TIME: 30 minutes.

HEALTHY HALIBUT CHOWDER

This dish has all the flavor of a traditional chowder with much less fat.

Ingredients

2 shallots, diced
2 stalks celery, diced
1 carrot, diced
1 tbsp olive oil
2 cloves garlic, minced
½ tsp salt
¼ tsp black pepper
¼ tsp paprika
¼ tsp thyme
2 bay leaves
1 cup dry white wine
2 cups fish stock (chicken stock can be substituted)
1 cup skim milk
2 potatoes, peeled and diced
2 tbsp cornstarch mixed with 2 tbsp cold milk
2 lbs halibut filet, cut into 1-inch chunks
Salt and pepper to taste
Fresh parsley, chopped for garnish

GLUTEN FREE

Cooking Instructions

Sauté the shallots, carrot and celery in the oil in a large stockpot set over medium heat until fragrant, about 5 minutes. Add the garlic, salt, pepper, paprika, thyme and bay leaves, and cook for 2 minutes, stirring constantly. Deglaze the pan with the white wine and reduce by half. Add the stock and milk, and bring to a simmer. Add the potatoes and cook until tender, about 10 minutes. Thicken with the cornstarch slurry and cook until the starch taste disappears, about 5 minutes. Add the halibut and cook until just done, about 5-7 minutes longer. Taste the chowder and adjust seasonings as necessary with salt and pepper. Garnish with fresh parsley.

Chef's Note:

Thickening with a cornstarch slurry can not only make any soup healthier (as opposed to thickening with a butter-based roux), but it also makes it gluten free!

Serves 6 – 8 | PREP TIME: 15 minutes. COOK TIME: 35 minutes.

CAJUN CRAWFISH CHOWDER

A lively chowder featuring all the bold flavors you'd expect in Cajun cooking along with a bit of cream to add richness and character.

Ingredients

½ lb bacon

1 large red onion, diced

1 green pepper, diced

2 stalks celery, diced

2 tbsp butter

2 cloves garlic, minced

½ tsp salt

¼ tsp cayenne pepper

¼ tsp paprika

¼ tsp oregano

1 cup dry white wine

32 oz fish stock

2 medium red potatoes, peeled and diced

1 lb crawfish tails, cleaned

1 cup corn kernels, fresh or frozen

1 tbsp cornstarch mixed with 1 tbsp cold milk

1 cup heavy cream

Salt and pepper to taste

Cooking Instructions

Cook the bacon in a large stockpot set over medium heat until browned and crispy, about 10 minutes. Remove bacon to drain on paper towels and then crumble. Add the butter to the pan and sauté the onion, green pepper and celery until fragrant, about 5 minutes. Add the garlic, salt, cayenne pepper, paprika and oregano, and cook for 2 minutes, stirring constantly. Deglaze the pan with the white wine and reduce by half. Add the stock and bring to a simmer. Add the potatoes and cook until tender, about 10 minutes. Add the crawfish, corn and crumbled bacon, and cook until the crawfish tails are warmed through, about 10 minutes longer. Thicken with the cornstarch slurry, making sure to cook out the starch taste, about 5 minutes longer. Stir in the heavy cream and immediately remove from heat. Taste and adjust seasonings as necessary with salt and pepper.

GLUTEN FREE

Serves 4 | PREP TIME: 15 minutes. COOK TIME: 30 minutes.

CREOLE SHRIMP BISQUE

A great soup to serve in a bread bowl for guests because it looks and tastes fantastic. If you love shrimp, that is.

Ingredients

2 shallots, diced
1 green pepper, diced
2 stalks celery, diced
1 tbsp olive
2 cloves garlic, minced
½ tsp salt
¼ tsp cayenne pepper
¼ tsp paprika
¼ tsp thyme
¼ tsp oregano
1 tbsp tomato paste
2 bay leaves
1 cup dry white wine
24 oz fish stock (chicken stock can be substituted)
2 tbsp cornstarch mixed with 2 tbsp cold milk
1 ½ lbs jumbo raw shrimp, shelled and cleaned
8 oz heavy cream
Salt and pepper to taste
Fresh parsley, chopped for garnish

GLUTEN FREE

Cooking Instructions

Sauté the shallots, green pepper and celery in the oil in a large stockpot set over medium heat until fragrant, about 5 minutes. Add the garlic, salt, cayenne pepper, paprika, thyme, oregano, tomato paste and bay leaves, and cook for 2 minutes, stirring constantly. Deglaze the pan with the white wine and reduce by half. Add the stock, bring to a simmer and then cook for 10 minutes to allow the flavors to develop. Thicken with the cornstarch slurry and cook until the starch taste disappears, about 5 minutes longer. I recommend pulsing this with an immersion blender to make the soup smoother. Add the shrimp and cook until they curl, turn pink and are just done, about 5-7 minutes. Stir in the heavy cream and remove immediately from heat. Taste and adjust seasonings as necessary with salt and pepper. Garnish with fresh parsley and serve.

Chef's Note:

Blend this entire soup with the immersion blender so it's silky smooth as a bisque should be.

Serves 6 | PREP TIME: 15 minutes. COOK TIME: 35 minutes.

BIG OCCASION BOUILLABAISSE

This recipe takes some time but is well worth it for a special occasion. Break out the nice china and candles, and open a bottle of good wine. Tonight you're getting fancy!

Ingredients

2 shallots, diced

2 leeks, root and top greens removed, sliced

1 head fennel, thinly sliced with fronds reserved for garnish

2 stalks celery, diced

2 tbsp olive oil

2 cloves garlic, minced

½ tsp salt

¼ tsp white pepper

¼ tsp paprika

¼ tsp thyme

2 bay leaves

¼ tsp red chili flakes

2 cups dry white wine

¼ tsp saffron

64 oz fish stock

3 tomatoes, chopped

1 lb firm white fleshed fish such as swordfish, monkfish and/or cod, cut into 1-inch chunks

½ lb clams, scrubbed and soaked for 20 minutes in fresh cold water to get the grit out

½ lb mussels, scrubbed, debearded and soaked for 20 minutes in fresh cold water to get the grit out

½ lb shrimp, shelled and cleaned

Salt and pepper to taste

Fennel fronds to garnish

Note: Don't forget to put the mussels and clams in cold water for 20 minutes to get the grit out.

Cooking Instructions

Sauté the shallots, leeks, fennel and celery in the canola oil in a large stockpot set over medium heat until fragrant, about 5 minutes. Add the garlic, salt, pepper, paprika, thyme, bay leaves and chili flakes to the pot. Cook for 2 minutes, stirring constantly. Deglaze the pan with the white wine and reduce by half. Add the saffron, stock and tomatoes, and bring to a simmer. Add the fish filets and cook until just done, about 5 minutes. Add the clams and mussels, and cook until they open, about 5-7 minutes longer. Finally add the shrimp and cook until pink and curled, about 5 minutes. Taste the bouillabaisse and adjust seasonings as necessary with salt and pepper. Garnish with fennel fronds.

Chef's Note:

For a large party, you can remove the seafood to a platter and serve the broth alongside. For individual servings, ladle the seafood into equal portions in bowls and then top with broth.

You can serve this dish with crostini which are traditionally spread with a rouille, a homemade mayonnaise mixed with a bit more saffron and some tomato paste. Here's the recipe:

1 cup mayonnaise
Pinch of saffron threads
1 tbsp tomato paste
1 tsp red chili flakes

GLUTEN
FREE

Serves 8 | PREP TIME: 30 minutes. COOK TIME: 45 minutes.

CURRIED SHRIMP SOUP WITH MANGO

In this well-balanced Asian soup, pungent curry powder and sharp lemongrass meet a nice sweet mango. It's a nice and refreshingly different flavor combination and a hearty soup, more like a spicy stew.

Ingredients

1 large red onion, diced
4 stalks celery, sliced
2 tbsp olive oil
2 cloves garlic, minced
1 one inch piece fresh ginger, peeled and sliced
½ tsp salt
1 tbsp mild yellow curry powder (unless you want it really spicy)
¼ tsp ground allspice
½ tsp cumin
1 stalk lemongrass, pounded and cut into 1 inch pieces
¼ tsp pepper
32oz fish stock
1 tbsp brown sugar
1 tbsp Worcestershire sauce
2 fresh ripe mangoes, peeled and diced
2 lbs jumbo raw shrimp, shelled and cleaned
Salt and pepper to taste
Sliced fresh scallions for garnish

Cooking Instructions

Sauté the onion and celery in the olive oil in a large stockpot set over medium heat until fragrant, about 5 minutes. Add the garlic, ginger, salt, curry powder, allspice, cumin, lemongrass and pepper, and cook for 2 minutes, stirring constantly. Add the stock, brown sugar and Worcestershire sauce, and bring to a simmer. Add the diced mango and cook for 15 minutes. Add the shrimp and cook until they curl, turn pink and are just done, about 5-7 minutes. Remove from the heat and adjust seasonings as necessary with salt and pepper.

Serve soup in large deep bowls, measuring 4-5 shrimp per bowl. Garnish with scallions.

Serves 8 | PREP TIME: 15 minutes. COOK TIME: 30 minutes.

INDONESIAN CRAB SOUP WITH LEMONGRASS

This soup is the perfect blend of rich flavor and sweetness without the price tag of lobster. It comes together quickly with just a few ingredients, but it's a knockout dish that can be served as a first course or stand-alone entrée.

Ingredients

2 shallots, diced

1 stalk celery, sliced

1 carrot, diced

1 tbsp olive oil

2 cloves garlic, minced

1 1-inch piece fresh ginger, peeled and diced

1 tbsp tomato paste

½ tsp salt

¼ tsp white pepper

32 oz fish stock

1 stalk lemongrass, smashed and cut into 2-inch pieces

1 lb crab meat, (preferably from Dungeness crab), picked over to remove shell pieces

Salt and pepper to taste

Sliced fresh scallions for garnish

GLUTEN FREE

Cooking Instructions

Sauté the shallot, celery and carrot in the olive oil in a large stockpot set over medium heat until fragrant, about 5 minutes. Add the garlic, ginger, tomato paste, salt and pepper, and cook for 2 minutes, stirring constantly. Add the stock and lemongrass, and bring to a simmer. Cook for 15 minutes to allow the flavors to develop. Add the crab meat and warm through, about 5 minutes. Remove from the heat and adjust seasonings as necessary with salt and pepper.

Chef's Note:

Whole crabs can be used in this recipe, and it's even better that way. Increase the fish stock to 48 ounces and add the cleaned crabs directly to the pot. Then increase the simmer time to 25 minutes. Remove the cooked crabs and allow to cool before removing the meat and adding it back into the soup.

Serves 4 | PREP TIME: 15 minutes. COOK TIME: 20 minutes.

CLASSIC SHE-CRAB SOUP

This wonderful recipe comes from the southeastern coast of America, but it's famous all over the country. Traditionally, it was made from only female crabs. People thought the meat from the smaller females was sweeter. Crab roe used to be included but in an effort to reduce the impact on crab populations, we now omit it. The touch of sherry at the end really sets off the richness.

Ingredients

4 tbsp butter
2 shallots, diced
2 stalks celery, diced
2 cloves garlic, minced
½ tsp salt
¼ tsp mace
¼ tsp paprika
¼ tsp thyme
¼ tsp pepper
3 tbsp flour
16 oz fish stock
16 oz milk
1 tbsp tomato paste
1 lb crab meat, shelled and cleaned
8 oz heavy cream
Salt and pepper to taste
4 tbsp dry sherry

Cooking Instructions

Melt the butter in a large stockpot set over medium heat. Sauté the shallots and celery in the butter until fragrant, about 5 minutes. Add the garlic, salt, mace, paprika, thyme and pepper, and cook for 2 minutes, stirring constantly. Add the flour and cook for another 5 minutes, stirring constantly so the roux doesn't burn. Pour in the stock and milk all at once, and bring to a simmer. Add tomato paste. Cook for 15 minutes to thicken the soup. Add the crab and warm through, about 5 minutes. Remove from the heat and stir in the cream. Adjust seasonings as necessary with salt and pepper.

Ladle into bowls and top each bowl with a spoonful of sherry.

Chef's Note:

Omitting the roe changes the soup dramatically, but it's what must be done to protect the crab populations.

Serves 4 | PREP TIME: 15 minutes. COOK TIME: 30 minutes.

HOT & SOUR SOUP (TOM YUM)

Tom Yum is a flavorful and warming Thai soup that's become popular all over the world. Though sourcing ingredients can be tricky, the soup is super quick, simple to make and very delicious. Serve this with a salad as a nice balanced lunch.

Ingredients

32 oz chicken stock

1 1-inch piece fresh ginger, peeled and sliced

2 cloves garlic, minced

1 stalk lemongrass, pounded and sliced into 2-inch pieces

3 Thai bird chiles, crushed

4 oz mushrooms, sliced (note: canned straw mushrooms can be used)

2 tbsp fish sauce

1 tbsp chili sauce

½ tsp salt

4 kaffir lime leaves

1 lb jumbo raw shrimp, shelled and cleaned

4 tbsp lime juice

Minced fresh scallions and cilantro leaves for garnish

Cooking Instructions

Heat the chicken broth in a large stockpot set over medium heat for 5 minutes. Add the ginger, garlic, lemongrass and Thai bird chiles, and bring to a simmer. Add the mushrooms, fish sauce, chili sauce, salt and kaffir lime leaves, and cook for 15 minutes. Add the shrimp and cook until they curl, turn pink and are just done, about 5-7 minutes. Remove from the heat, add the lime juice and adjust seasonings as necessary with salt and pepper. Garnish with scallions and cilantro, and serve.

Chef's Note:

The hard-to-get ingredients can be found at specialty stores online or at your local Asian market. To find the spices, you can visit The Spice House, (they have a few in the Midwest) with a strong online presence.

Serves 4 | PREP TIME: 10 minutes. COOK TIME: 25 minutes.

SWEET & SOUR FISH STEW

This stew is loaded with fresh fish and vegetables kicked up with lime juice, ginger, cilantro, and pineapple. Serve with a cucumber salad and a sparkling water for a great light lunch.

Ingredients

2 shallots, diced

2 stalks celery, diced

1 tbsp canola oil

1 tbsp butter

2 cloves garlic, minced

1 1-inch piece fresh ginger, peeled and diced

1 stalk lemongrass, pounded and cut into 1-inch pieces

32 oz fish stock

1 tbsp fish sauce

2 tbsp honey

2 cups fresh pineapple, diced

½ tsp salt

¼ tsp white pepper

1 lb firm white fish filets, like catfish, walleye or whitefish, cut into bite-sized pieces

Salt and pepper to taste

Cooking Instructions

Sauté the shallots and celery in the canola oil and butter in a large stockpot set over medium heat until fragrant, about 5 minutes. Add the garlic, ginger and lemongrass, and cook for 2 minutes, stirring constantly. Add the stock, fish sauce, honey, pineapple, salt and pepper, and bring to a simmer. Cook for 10 minutes to allow the flavors to develop. Add the fish and cook until just done, about 5-7 minutes. Remove from the heat and adjust seasonings as necessary with salt and pepper.

Serves 4 | PREP TIME: 10 minutes. COOK TIME: 25 minutes.

SHRIMP SOBA NOODLE SOUP

Soba noodles are made from buckwheat and served all over Japan.

Ingredients

1 lb jumbo raw shrimp, shelled and cleaned

1 tsp Chinese five-spice powder

¼ cup mirin

2 tsp honey

¼ cup soy sauce

1 small yellow onion, diced

1 carrot, diced

1 tbsp olive oil

2 cloves garlic, minced

1 one inch piece fresh ginger, peeled and sliced

½ tsp salt

¼ tsp white pepper

32 oz chicken stock

3-4 stalks bok choy, sliced with larger leaves included (about ½ a head)

Salt and pepper to taste

1 lb soba noodles

Sliced fresh scallions for garnish

Cooking Instructions

Heat 2 quarts of salted water in a large pot to boil the soba noodles.

Take the cleaned shrimp and dust them with the five-spice powder. Mix the mirin, honey and soy sauce in a bowl, and add the shrimp to marinate while you make the rest of the soup.

Sauté the onion and carrot in the olive oil in a large stockpot set over medium heat until fragrant, about 5 minutes. Add the garlic, ginger, salt and pepper, and cook for 2 minutes, stirring constantly. Add the stock and bring to a simmer. Add the bok choy and cook for 3 minutes. Add the shrimp including the marinade and cook until they curl, turn pink and are just done, about 5-7 minutes. Remove from the heat and adjust seasonings as necessary with salt and pepper.

Boil the soba noodles according to package directions. When the noodles are finished ladle the noodles into four bowls. Top with the hot soup, measuring 4-5 shrimp per bowl. Garnish with scallions and serve.

Serves 4 | PREP TIME: 15 minutes. COOK TIME: 25 minutes.

ABALONE SOUP WITH STRAW MUSHROOMS, GINGER & RICE NOODLES

Abalone can be difficult to source these days due to overharvesting, but you can find some online. The pounding and long cooking time is necessary to tenderize the abalone. Do not try to rush this process or the abalone will end up with the a texture of a bicycle tire! If cooked properly, it's great, tender, and delicious. You can serve this with ice mint tea or Kirin Ichiban and a simple salad with sesame ginger dressing.

Ingredients

1 lb jumbo raw shrimp, shelled and cleaned

4 oz dried straw mushrooms, reconstituted and chopped

1 carrot, finely diced

1 head bok choy, sliced (leaves included)

1 1-inch piece of ginger, peeled and diced

2 tbsp canola oil

1 clove garlic, minced

1 tsp salt

½ tsp white pepper

32 oz chicken stock

1 lb abalone, thawed, sliced, pounded and cut into 1-inch pencil thin strips (substitute canned abalone if necessary)

8 oz rice noodles

6 scallions, thinly sliced for garnish

Bring 2 quarts of water to a simmer in a large pot for cooking the noodles.

Note: You need to reconstitute the mushrooms which takes about 30 minutes (see Cook's Note).

Cooking Instructions

In a separate stockpot, sauté the reconstituted mushrooms, carrot, bok choy and ginger in the canola oil for 5 minutes over high heat. Add the garlic, salt and white pepper, and cook for one minute. Add the chicken stock and bring to a simmer. Add the abalone and cook, covered, for 1 hour. Check the texture of the abalone. If it is still rubbery, cover and cook for another 30 minutes; otherwise, remove the soup from the heat and cover. Cook the rice noodles according to package directions then divide them evenly among six bowls. Ladle the hot soup over the noodles and top with scallions.

Chef's Note:

To reconstitute dry mushrooms add boiling water to a bowl and soak the mushrooms for 20-30 minutes. The resulting broth is quite flavorful and can be added to the soup if desired.

Serves 6 | PREP TIME: 15 minutes. COOK TIME: 1½ hours.

TUNISIAN FISH CHOWDER

This recipe is a great example of how simple humble ingredients combine to make something wonderful. It is light and full of clean flavors and will have your family and friends asking for seconds! Don't tell them how easy it was to make.

Ingredients

1 medium onion, chopped

1 small fennel bulb, sliced

2 stalks celery, sliced (leaves included)

2 tbsp olive oil

2 cloves garlic, minced

1 tsp salt

1 tsp harissa

½ tsp cumin

½ tsp paprika

40 oz fish stock

4 medium red skinned potatoes, washed and cut into ½ inch chunks

1 pinch saffron

3 medium tomatoes, chopped

1 lb firm white fleshed fish fillets such as cod or haddock, cut into 1-inch chunks

1 lb squid, cleaned and cut into ½ inch chunks

Juice from 1 lemon

½ cup fresh parsley, chopped

½ cup fresh cilantro, chopped

Salt and pepper to taste

Cooking Instructions

Sauté the onion, fennel and celery in the olive oil in a large stockpot set over medium heat until the onions are translucent, about 7-10 minutes. Add the garlic, salt, harissa, cumin and paprika. Cook for one minute, stirring constantly. Add the stock and potatoes. Bring to a simmer. Add the saffron and tomatoes. Cover and cook for 10 minutes to allow the flavors to develop and potatoes to soften. Add the fish and squid. Cook, uncovered, until the fish is just done and the potatoes are tender, about 10 minutes. Remove the pot from the heat and stir in the lemon juice and fresh herbs. Taste the chowder and adjust seasonings with salt and pepper as needed.

Serves 6 | PREP TIME: 20 minutes. COOK TIME: 30 minutes.

CHAPTER SIX

HEARTY STEWS AND CHILIS FROM ALL OVER THE MAP

A good stew sends terrific aromas throughout the house and gives your guests a warm greeting. It's just pure pleasure. And that's what stews are for; slow cooking meals with fantastic flavors melded together. The smells are pure joy.

A good browning is very important for the end flavor. Don't forget to get the pot hot before adding the oil. Do not crowd the pan. Brown in batches. Your browning shouldn't take more than two minutes a side. Then you can simmer away with the confidence you are about to serve a delicious and hearty meal.

Stews can make the ideal dinner choice for any occasion. In this chapter, you'll have plenty of deliciousness to choose from. You'll be able to pick your favorite dish and make it special for you, your family, and your friends, so you'll be able to have a traditional home cooked meal ready for everyone to enjoy for dinner.

HEARTY BEEF STEW

Slow-cooked beef and potatoes with carrots, celery, peas and a touch of onion;
it's the quintessential classic for a cold winter's night.
Served with a nice loaf of crusty bread or fresh buttermilk biscuits...heaven!

Ingredients

2 lbs beef stew meat, trimmed of fat and cut into 1-inch cubes
1 tsp salt
1 tsp freshly ground black pepper
2 tbsp olive oil
1 medium onion, diced
2 stalks celery, diced
2 carrots, sliced
4 cloves garlic, minced
2 tbsp tomato paste
½ tsp granulated sugar
2 bay leaves
1 tsp thyme
1 cup apple juice
24 oz beef stock
1 tbsp Worcestershire sauce
3 potatoes, cut into ½ inch chunks
1 cup peas, fresh or frozen
2 tbsp cornstarch mixed with 2 tbsp cold milk
Salt and pepper to taste

Cooking Instructions

Warm the oil in a large stockpot over medium heat. Toss the beef with the salt and pepper and brown the beef in 1 tablespoon of hot oil in two batches, about 5 minutes a batch. Remove the browned beef to a large bowl and set aside. Sauté the onion, celery and carrot in the same pot with the other tablespoon of oil set over medium heat until fragrant, about 5 minutes. Add the garlic, tomato paste, sugar and dried spices. Cook for two minutes, stirring constantly. Deglaze the pan with the apple juice and reduce by half. Add the beef stew meat, stock and Worcestershire sauce to the pot and bring the stew to a simmer. Cover the pot, turn heat to low and cook until the beef is tender, about 1 hour. Add the potatoes and peas, then cook for another 30 minutes. Thicken the stew using the cornstarch slurry, adding it slowly and cooking for another 5 minutes to make sure the starchy taste is cooked out. Add less of the slurry for a thinner stew. Taste and adjust seasonings as necessary with salt and pepper.

Chef's Note:

While browning meat seems pretty straightforward, people often don't quite get it right, and a good browning makes a big difference in the final taste. Make sure to use a heavy-bottomed pot. Let it heat up to medium high. Wait until the oil is heated, you see ripples in it and is as close to smoking, without smoking, as you can get it. Be careful not to crowd the pan with meat, which will cool the bottom of the pot too much too fast. Also, let the meat sit on one side and get good, deep-brown edges before turning. Those little bits of caramelized meat add a nice savory flavor to the dish.

Serves 8 | PREP TIME: 20 minutes. COOK TIME: about 2 hours.

BRUNSWICK STEW

The origin of this recipe is highly disputed between Virginia and the Carolinas, with each state having a Brunswick County that claims ownership. No matter the true origins, the slow-cooked combination of smoked ham, sausage, and chicken with hearty okra, corn, and butter beans is perfect when the snow is blowing sideways. Serve with freshly baked biscuits.

Ingredients

1 large Vidalia onion, chopped

2 stalks celery, diced

1 green pepper, diced

2 tbsp butter

1 tbsp canola oil

8 oz Andouille sausage, cut into thin coins

3 cloves garlic, minced

½ tsp salt

2 bay leaves

1 tsp paprika

1 tsp parsley

1 tsp thyme

1 tsp freshly ground black pepper

1 lb smoked ham steak, cubed

4 chicken legs or thighs

4 large tomatoes, peeled, seeded and chopped

48 oz chicken stock

2 cups shelled butter beans

1 tbsp brown sugar

1 tbsp Worcestershire sauce

1 cup frozen chopped okra, thawed

1 cup corn, fresh or frozen

Salt and pepper to taste

Cooking Instructions

Melt the butter with the oil in a large stockpot set over medium-high heat. Sauté the onion, celery and green pepper until fragrant, about 5 minutes. Add the sausage, garlic, salt, and dried spices. Cook for 2 minutes, stirring constantly. Add the smoked ham steak, chicken legs, tomatoes and stock. Bring to a simmer and add the butter beans. Cover the pot and continue cooking until the chicken is cooked through and beans are tender, about 30-40 minutes. Remove the chicken, let cool, then shred the meat from the legs and return it to the pot. Add the brown sugar and Worcestershire sauce along with the okra and corn. Cook for an additional 8 minutes. Taste the soup and adjust seasonings with salt and pepper as necessary.

Chef's Note:

This stew is great made with all manner of meats.

Serves 8 | PREP TIME: 20 minutes. COOK TIME: 1 hour.

CABBAGE & SMOKED SAUSAGE STEW

This recipe is simple, quick, and deeply satisfying. The smoky sausage simply paired with cabbage and potatoes is a nice reminder that things don't have to be complicated to be cherished and good.

Ingredients

1 onion, chopped
1 stalk celery, diced
1 carrot, sliced
1 tbsp olive oil
1 lb smoked sausage such as kielbasa, cut into ½ inch chunks
½ tsp salt
2 cloves garlic, minced
1 bay leaf
½ tsp thyme
½ tsp freshly ground black pepper
32 oz chicken stock
2 large potatoes, cut into ½ inch chunks
1 head green cabbage, cubed
1 tbsp red wine vinegar
Salt and pepper to taste

GLUTEN FREE

Cooking Instructions

Sauté the onion, celery and carrot in the olive oil in a large stockpot set over medium heat until fragrant, about 5 minutes. Add the sausage, salt, garlic and dried spices. Cook for two minutes, stirring constantly. Add the stock and bring to a simmer. Add the potatoes and cabbage, and turn the heat to low. Cover and continue cooking until everything is tender, about 20-30 minutes. Stir in the vinegar. Taste the soup and adjust seasonings with salt and pepper as necessary.

Serves 6-8 | PREP TIME: 10 minutes. COOK TIME: 35 minutes.

CHORIZO & SWEET-POTATO STEW

Years ago, sweet potatoes hit the mainstream. All the papers and magazines were touting the remarkable nutritional benefits of this delectable tuber. Its strong distinctive flavor, can be hard to pair with many soups. A hearty stew paired with this bold, spicy sausage created a real stick-to-your-ribs dish.

Ingredients

1 lb Spanish chorizo, cut into ¼ inch thick coins

1 medium onion, halved and sliced

2 medium carrots, halved and sliced

3 cloves garlic, minced

½ tsp salt

½ tsp paprika

½ tsp thyme

24 oz chicken stock

2 lbs sweet potatoes, peeled and quartered

Salt and pepper to taste

Yogurt, sour cream or crème fraîche for garnish

Chives, chopped for garnish

GLUTEN FREE

Cooking Instructions

Sauté the chorizo coins over medium-low heat in a large stockpot, about 5-8 minutes so the chorizo has rendered and crisped a bit. Remove it from the stockpot and set aside. Add the onions and carrots to the pot, increase the heat to medium high and sauté until translucent, about 8 minutes longer. Add the garlic, salt, paprika and thyme. Cook for one minute, stirring constantly. Add the chicken broth and sweet potatoes. Bring the stew to a simmer, cover the pot and turn the heat to low. Cook for 30 minutes or until the sweet potatoes are tender. Stir in the chorizo. Cook for another 5 minutes to allow the flavors to marry. Taste stew and adjust seasonings as necessary with salt and pepper. Put in serving bowls and garnish with a dollop of yogurt, sour cream or crème fraîche, and chives.

Serves 6-8 | PREP TIME: 10 minutes. COOK TIME: 45 minutes.

COCK-A-LEEKIE STEW

This is a version of a classic Scottish soup of chicken and leeks.
This recipe has pearled barley, celery, and carrots to turn.

Ingredients

5 leeks, root and green tops trimmed and cut into ¼ inch half moons

2 carrots, sliced

2 stalks celery, sliced

½ tsp salt

4 tbsp butter

3 cloves garlic, sliced

½ tsp marjoram

½ tsp thyme

¼ tsp chervil

¼ tsp rosemary

32 oz water

1 roasting chicken cut into 8 pieces (about 4 lbs)

4 oz pearled barley

Salt and black pepper to taste

Cooking Instructions

Sauté the leeks, celery and carrots with the salt in the butter over medium-low heat in a large stockpot until fragrant, about 10 minutes. Add the garlic and dried herbs. Cook for 2 minutes, stirring constantly. Add the water and chicken. Bring to a simmer, cover and cook for 30 minutes. Remove the lid and skim any fat or froth from the top of the stew with a ladle. Add the pearled barley and recover the pot. Cook for another 30 minutes until the barley is tender. Remove the chicken from the stew, let cool and then debone it, leaving the chicken in large 1-inch chunks. Return the chicken to the stew, taste and adjust seasonings with salt and pepper as needed.

Serves 4–6 | PREP TIME: 20 minutes. COOK TIME: 1 hour.

SMOKED SALMON STEW

Ingredients

½ lb bacon
4 tbsp butter
3 tbsp flour
1 large red onion, diced
2 stalks celery, diced
2 cloves garlic, minced
½ tsp salt
¼ tsp cayenne pepper
¼ tsp paprika
¼ tsp thyme
¼ tsp tarragon
1 cup dry white wine
24 oz fish stock
2 medium red potatoes, peeled and diced
1 lb smoked salmon
1 cup English peas, fresh or frozen
1 cup heavy cream
Salt and pepper to taste

Cooking Instructions

Cook the bacon in a large stockpot set over medium heat until browned and crispy, about 10 minutes. Remove bacon to drain on paper towels and then crumble. Add the butter, and sauté the onion and celery until fragrant, about 5 minutes. Add the flour and cook for 3 minutes, stirring constantly. Add the garlic, salt, cayenne pepper, paprika, thyme and tarragon, and cook for 2 minutes, stirring constantly. Add the wine and stock. Bring to a simmer, add the potatoes and cook until tender, about 10 minutes. Add the smoked salmon, peas and crumbled bacon. Cook until warmed through, about 10 minutes longer. Stir in the heavy cream and remove immediately from the heat. Taste and adjust seasonings as necessary with salt and pepper.

Serves 4 | PREP TIME: 15 minutes. COOK TIME: 30 minutes.

RED BEAN CHICKEN CHILI

Ingredients

1 large onion, diced

2 stalks celery, diced

6 cups tomatoes, chopped OR 3 (14.5 ounce)
cans diced tomatoes

2 cloves garlic, minced

1 tbsp ground cumin

4 tbsp chile powder

2 cups cooked chicken, cubed

1 cup cooked red beans

1 tbsp canola oil

16 oz chicken stock

Salt and pepper to taste

Cooking Instructions

Warm the oil in a stockpot over medium heat. Add the onion and celery and sauté until softened, about 10 minutes. Add the garlic and the spices and cook until fragrant (about one minute) then add the tomatoes and the chicken stock. Bring to a simmer and cook for 15 minutes. Add the beans and the chicken. Return to a simmer and cook another 30 minutes to allow flavors to develop and chili to thicken. Taste and add salt or pepper as needed. Garnish as desired.

Serves 4 | PREP TIME: 15 minutes. COOK TIME: 60 minutes.

THAI COCONUT SHRIMP CURRY

This classic Thai-inspired curry with a coconut-milk base offers lots of fresh bright flavors in an easy-to-make and spicy stew served over rice.

Ingredients

1 small yellow onion, diced

2 cloves garlic, minced

2 tbsp canola oil

1 1-inch piece fresh ginger, peeled and diced

2 tbsp red curry paste

½ tsp salt

¼ tsp white pepper

1 can coconut milk

1 tbsp fish sauce

1 lb jumbo raw shrimp, shelled and cleaned

Salt and pepper to taste

3 scallions, sliced for garnish

Cooking Instructions

Sauté the onion and garlic in the canola oil in a large stockpot set over medium-high heat until lightly golden, about 3 minutes. Add the ginger, curry paste, salt and pepper to the pot and cook for 2 minutes, stirring constantly. Add the coconut milk and whisk to incorporate. Bring to a simmer. Once a simmer is reached add the fish sauce and cook for 5 minutes. The soup will begin to thicken. Add the shrimp and cook until they curl and turn pink and are just done, about 5-7 minutes. Remove from the heat and adjust seasonings as necessary with salt and pepper. Garnish with scallions and serve over rice.

Serves 4 | PREP TIME: 15 minutes. COOK TIME: 25 minutes.

DELICIOUS FARRO & CANNELLINI BEAN STEW

Farro is a wheat grain similar to barley, spelt or wheat berries and super nutritious. It gives body to soups or salads. Serve with a big salad dressed with an acidic vinaigrette to set off the earthy flavors of the beans and grains.

Ingredients

2 leeks, root and top greens removed, sliced

1 green pepper, diced

1 carrot, diced

2 stalks celery, diced

1 tbsp olive oil

½ tsp salt

¼ tsp black pepper

2 cloves garlic, minced

2 tbsp tomato paste

1 bay leaf

½ tsp rosemary

¼ tsp oregano

2 medium tomatoes, chopped

48 oz vegetable stock

½ cup farro, rinsed

2 cups dry cannellini beans, soaked overnight in salted water

Note: You'll need to soak the beans overnight.

Cooking Instructions

Sauté the leeks, green pepper, carrots and celery in the olive oil in a large stockpot set over medium heat until fragrant, about 5 minutes. Add the salt, pepper, garlic, the tomato paste, bay leaf, rosemary and oregano to the pot and cook for two minutes, stirring constantly. Add the tomatoes and the vegetable stock to the pot and bring the soup to a simmer. Once a simmer is reached add the farro and the cannellini beans and cook until both are tender, about 30-40 minutes. Taste the soup and adjust seasonings as necessary with salt and pepper.

Serves 6 | PREP TIME: 10 minutes. COOK TIME: 50 minutes.

COLORADO GREEN CHILI

Feel free to double on the jalapeño and serranos if you like to heat things up. You can serve this with freshly baked corn bread and honey butter to help fight back the flames.

Ingredients

2 large poblano peppers, roasted

2 jalapeño peppers, roasted

1 serrano pepper, roasted

10 New Mexico hatch green chiles, roasted

2 tbsp butter

2 tbsp canola oil

2 lbs boneless pork roast or butt cut into 1 inch chunks

1 tsp salt

1 tsp cumin

1 large red onion, chopped

2 carrots, chopped

2 stalks celery, chopped

4 cloves garlic, diced

1 bay leaf

½ tsp oregano

½ tsp white pepper

32 oz chicken stock

2 cups cooked pinto beans

Salt and pepper to taste

1 tbsp cornstarch mixed with 1 tbsp cold water

Cooking Instructions

Roast the chiles over a grill or open flame until blackened, 10 to 15 minutes. Remove to a large bowl and cover tightly for 30 minutes. Once cool, peel off the charred skins of the peppers, cut in half and remove all seeds. Chop the chiles and reserve. While the chiles rest and cool down prep the rest of the chili.

Melt the butter with the oil in a large stockpot set over medium-high heat. Sprinkle salt and cumin over pork. Brown the pork in batches, about 5 minutes a batch, and remove to a plate. Sauté the onion, carrots and celery in the stockpot until fragrant, about 5 minutes. Add the garlic and the dried spices and cook for two minutes, stirring constantly. Add the chicken stock, chopped chiles and the pork to the pot and bring to a simmer. Once a simmer is reached cover the pot and turn heat to low. Cook for 45 minutes or until the pork is tender, stirring occasionally. Once the pork is tender add the beans and continue to cook until warmed through. Taste and adjust seasonings as necessary with salt and pepper. Add the cornstarch slurry a little at a time to thicken as desired.

Chef's Note:

You can cook this dish in a slow cooker. Here's what to do:

Rub the butter onto the bottom and sides of the slow cooker. Lay the pork pieces in the bottom, and then sprinkle in the spices. Layer the chopped chiles, carrot, onion, celery, and garlic. Top with the stock and cook on low heat for 8 hours. Add the beans, warm through and serve.

Serves 6-8 | PREP TIME: 20 minutes. COOK TIME: 1 hour.

ROADHOUSE BEEF CHILI

An extra meaty and hearty version of Beef Chili.

Ingredients

2 lbs ground beef, 80% lean

1 large onion, diced

2 stalks celery, diced

1 tbsp canola oil

2 cloves garlic, minced

1 tbsp ground cumin

4 tbsp chili powder

6 cups tomatoes, chopped or 3 (14.5 ounce) cans diced tomatoes

2 tbsp tomato paste

16 ounces beef stock

2 cups cooked dark red kidney beans

Salt and pepper to taste

Cooking Instructions

Brown the ground beef in a heavy skillet for 5-7 minutes, and drain well. Warm the oil in a large stockpot over medium heat, add the onion and celery. Sauté until softened, about 10 minutes. Add the garlic, cumin and 2 tablespoons of the chili powder. Cook until fragrant, about one minute, then add the tomatoes, tomato paste and beef stock. Bring to a simmer and cook for 15 minutes. Add the kidney beans and beef. Return to a simmer and cook another 40-60 minutes to allow flavors to develop and chili to thicken. If you are short on time, I've served this after 30 minutes of cooking, and it still tastes great but has more liquid. Add the remaining 2 tablespoons of chili powder 15 minutes before service to underscore the flavors. Taste and add salt or pepper as needed.

Chef's Note:

The finish, when you add a second round of spice just before serving, is called "the second dump" in competitions. It's a tried-and-true secret for brightening the flavors.

Serves 6 | PREP TIME: 20 minutes. COOK TIME: 90 minutes.

HEART-HEALTHY VEGETARIAN CHILI

This fast and easy recipe proves you don't need meat to enjoy an authentic tasting and satisfying bowl of red. This recipe has crumbled soy protein (like tofu). You can garnish this with a bit of chopped onion and some shredded sharp cheddar cheese, unless you are going vegan, of course.

Ingredients

1 large red onion, diced
2 medium carrots, diced
2 stalks celery, diced
1 tbsp canola oil
2 cloves garlic, minced
2 tbsp tomato paste
1 chipotle chili, chopped
½ tsp oregano
½ tsp salt
½ tsp cumin
¼ tsp cayenne pepper
1 tsp chili powder
4 tomatoes, peeled and chopped
32 oz vegetable stock
8 oz crumbled soy protein
1 cup dark red kidney beans, cooked
1 zucchini, quartered and sliced
1 ear sweet corn, kernels cut from the cob
Salt and pepper to taste
1 tbsp cornstarch with 1 tbsp cold water

Cooking Instructions

Sauté the onion, carrot and celery in the oil in a large stockpot set over medium heat until fragrant, about 5 minutes. Add the garlic, tomato paste, chipotle, oregano, salt, cumin, cayenne and chili powder. Cook for 2 minutes, stirring constantly. Add the tomatoes and stock, and bring the soup to a simmer. Add the crumbled soy protein, kidney beans, zucchini and corn. Cover and cook for 20 minutes to allow the flavors to develop. Add the cornstarch slurry and cook an additional 5 minutes to allow the chili to thicken and cook out the starchy taste. Remove from the heat and stir in the corn. Taste the soup and adjust seasonings as necessary with salt and pepper.

Chef's Note:

If you cannot find crumbled soy feel free to substitute two diced Boca Burgers to similar soy based protein replacement.

VEGAN FAVORITE

GLUTEN FREE

Serves 4–6 | PREP TIME: 15 minutes. COOK TIME: 30 minutes.

POBLANO CHICKEN CHILI

The poblano peppers give this soup a bit of heat balanced by the fresh and cool flavors of tomatillos, avocado, and lime. Pinto beans add a bit of creaminess to finish it all off wonderfully for a nice variation on a traditional chili.

Ingredients

1 large red onion, diced
2 stalks of celery, diced
2 medium Poblano peppers, diced
8 medium tomatillos, husked, washed and chopped
1 tbsp olive oil
3 cloves garlic, minced
½ tsp salt
½ tsp cumin
¼ tsp paprika
¼ tsp black pepper
32 oz chicken stock
1 cup pinto beans, soaked in salted water overnight
1 lb roasted chicken, shredded
Salt and pepper to taste
2 avocados, diced
Fresh scallions, chopped and lime wedges for garnish

Note: You need to soak the pinto beans overnight.

Cooking Instructions

Sauté the onion, celery, poblano peppers and tomatillos in the olive oil in a large stockpot set over medium heat until the onions are translucent and the peppers are fragrant, about 8 minutes. Add the garlic, salt, cumin, paprika and pepper, and cook for two minutes, stirring constantly. Add the stock and beans, and bring to a simmer. Then cover the pot and turn the heat to low. Continue cooking until the beans are tender, about 35-45 minutes. Add the shredded chicken and warm through, about 3 minutes more. Taste and adjust seasonings as necessary with salt and pepper. Ladle the soup into large bowls and divide the diced avocado among them. Garnish with fresh scallions and serve with lime wedges.

Serves 4-6 | PREP TIME: 20 minutes. COOK TIME: 1 hour.

WHITE BEAN TURKEY CHILI

This turkey chili is light colored and very low fat. Top with
some shreds of sharp cheddar cheese and scallions,
and serve with oyster crackers on the side.

Ingredients

1 medium onion, diced

2 stalks celery, diced

1 yellow or orange pepper, diced

1 carrot, diced

1 tbsp canola oil

1 lb ground turkey breast

½ tsp salt

3 cloves garlic, minced

2 tsp chili powder

1 tsp cumin

½ tsp paprika

¼ tsp cayenne pepper

32 oz chicken stock

8 oz Great Northern white beans, cooked

1 tbsp cornstarch mixed with 1 tbsp cold milk

Salt and pepper to taste

GLUTEN
FREE

Cooking Instructions

Sauté the onion, celery, yellow pepper and carrot in the olive oil in a large
stockpot set over medium heat until fragrant, about 5 minutes. Add the ground
turkey and cook until done, using a spatula to break the meat up into small
chunks, about 10 minutes. Add the salt, garlic and dried spices. Cook for
2 minutes, stirring constantly. Add the stock and bring to a simmer. Cover the
pot and continue cooking until the flavors have married, about 20-30 minutes.
Remove the lid, add the cornstarch slurry and allow to thicken, about 5 minutes.
Taste the soup and adjust seasonings with salt and pepper as necessary.

Serves 4-6 | PREP TIME: 20 minutes. COOK TIME: 45 minutes.

DEEP SOUTH BURGOO

This rich and savory stew is a tradition unto itself in the South. Typically, burgoo is served for large occasions. It serves well over rice or with a nice loaf of crusty bread. This recipe is perfect to cook on a slow cooker, put everything together in the morning, and it's ready when you get home!

Ingredients

2 lbs beef stew meat, cut into 1-inch cubes

2 lbs lamb stew meat, cut into 1-inch cubes

1 tsp salt

1 tsp freshly ground black pepper

2 tbsp olive oil

2 medium onions, diced

2 carrots, sliced

2 stalks celery, sliced

4 large tomatoes, peeled, seeded and chopped

2 cloves garlic, minced

32 oz beef stock

1 tbsp Worcestershire sauce

1 tsp hot sauce

1 tsp thyme

½ tsp marjoram

1 tsp brown sugar

½ head green cabbage, grated

2 cups corn kernels, fresh or frozen

1 lb fresh green beans, washed and cut into 1-inch pieces

Salt and pepper to taste

Note: This recipe requires a slow cooker.

Cooking Instructions

Toss the meats with the salt, pepper and olive oil in a large bowl and pour into to the slow cooker. Add the onions, carrots, celery, tomatoes, garlic, beef stock, Worcestershire sauce, hot sauce, dried herbs and brown sugar. Set the slow cooker to low heat and cook undisturbed for 8 hours. Remove the lid and add the cabbage, corn and green beans. Cook an additional 30 minutes until green beans are tender. Taste and adjust seasonings as needed with salt and pepper.

Serves 8 | PREP TIME: 10 minutes. COOK TIME: 8½ hours.

ISRAELI EGGPLANT STEW WITH COUSCOUS

This is a light stew, perfect for a summer evening. Feel free to substitute whatever vegetables you have on hand. In this dish, you cook the couscous right in the pot which saves time and adds body.

Ingredients

1 large onion, diced
1 carrot, diced
1 medium green pepper, diced
2 tbsp olive oil
3 cloves garlic, minced
½ tsp salt
½ tsp thyme
¼ tsp coriander
¼ tsp powdered ginger
Pinch of sugar
40 oz chicken stock
1 lb boneless skinless chicken breast, cubed
3 tomatoes, peelcd, seeded and chopped
2 medium eggplants, peeled and cut into 1-inch chunks
1 zucchini, cut into half moons
1 cup couscous
Salt and pepper black pepper to taste
Shredded fresh basil for garnish

Cooking Instructions

Sauté the onion, carrot and green pepper in the olive oil in a large stockpot over medium heat until translucent, about 10 minutes. Add the garlic and dried herbs. Cook for 1 minute while stirring. Add the chicken stock, chicken and tomatoes. Bring to a simmer, cover and cook for 20 minutes until the chicken is done. Add the eggplant and zucchini, and cook until tender, about 15 minutes. Remove from the heat and add the couscous. Stir to combine, cover the pot and do not disturb for 7 minutes. Remove the lid and adjust seasonings with salt and pepper as needed.

Ladle into bowls and top with finely shredded fresh basil and serve.

Serves 6 | PREP TIME: 15 minutes. COOK TIME: 45 minutes.

PERSIAN LAMB & SPINACH STEW

Very simple and easy, this stew is sure to satisfy. It has a little bit of curry powder from the Punjab area which has less cumin and a little more ginger for more subtle flavor.

Ingredients

1 carrot, sliced

2 leeks, root and green tops removed, sliced

3 tbsp butter

1 tbsp olive oil

4 cloves garlic

½ tsp salt

½ tsp red curry powder

½ tsp turmeric

¼ tsp Ceylon cinnamon

¼ tsp cayenne pepper

32 oz chicken stock

2 lbs lamb stew meat, cut into 1 inch pieces

2 bunches fresh spinach, washed and chopped (or 2 boxes frozen chopped spinach)

1 bunch flat-leaf parsley, washed and chopped

1 tbsp brown sugar

Salt and pepper to taste

1 tbsp lime juice

Cooking Instructions

Melt the butter in the oil in a large stockpot over medium-low heat. Add the carrot and leeks, and cook for 5 minutes. Add the garlic, salt, curry powder, turmeric, cinnamon and cayenne pepper. Continue cooking for 2 minutes, stirring constantly. Add the chicken stock and lamb, and bring to a simmer. Cover the stew, reduce the heat to low and cook until the lamb is tender, about 35 to 45 minutes. Add the spinach, parsley and brown sugar. Continue cooking for 10 minutes. Taste the stew and adjust the seasonings as necessary with salt and pepper. Remove from the heat and stir in the lime juice. Serve immediately.

GLUTEN FREE

Serves 6–8 | PREP TIME: 15 minutes. COOK TIME: 1 hour.

SLOW COOKER JAMBALAYA

Jambalaya has origins in Caribbean and Spanish cuisines, mixed up with some French Creole influence. This version of a hearty classic includes chicken and shrimp, is made in the slow cooker, and served over rice (cooked separately).

Ingredients

1 tbsp butter

1 lb Andouille sausage, cut into thin coins

1 lb boneless skinless chicken breast, cut into one inch chunks

1 large onion, diced

1 green pepper, diced

2 stalks celery, diced

2 cloves garlic, minced

½ tsp salt

¼ tsp thyme

¼ tsp cayenne pepper

¼ tsp paprika

¼ tsp oregano

16 oz chicken stock

½ lb jumbo shrimp, shelled and cleaned

Salt and pepper to taste

Fresh parsley for garnish

Note: This recipe requires a slow cooker.

Cooking Instructions

Run 1 tablespoon butter all over the inside of your slow cooker. Layer the Andouille sausage, chicken, onion, green pepper, and celery in the slow cooker. Mix the garlic, salt, thyme, cayenne, paprika and oregano with the chicken stock and add to the slow cooker. Set heat to low and cook for 8 hours. Once that time has passed remove the lid and stir. Add the shrimp and cook until they curl and turn pink and are just done, about 10 minutes longer. Taste and adjust seasonings as necessary with salt and pepper. Ladle the Jambalaya over rice in large bowls and garnish with fresh parsley.

Chef's Note:

Jambalaya is usually a multi-step hassle to prepare, but this recipe is simpler.

GLUTEN FREE

Serves 4 | PREP TIME: 15 minutes. COOK TIME: 8½ hours.

MASSAMAN CHICKEN CURRY STEW

Thai food delivers unique flavors and some of the most delicious in the world.
This hearty stew balances spice from yellow curry paste with the sweetness of coconut milk.
It can be served over rice or with warm flatbread.

Ingredients

1 medium onion, diced

2 carrots, sliced

1 tbsp olive oil

2 cloves garlic, minced

½ tsp salt

2 tbsp Massaman curry paste

1 inch piece of ginger, peeled and sliced into coins

¼ tsp white pepper

1 lb boneless skinless chicken breast, cut into large chunks

2 bay leaves

1 12 oz can of coconut milk

12 oz chicken stock

2 large potatoes, cut into big chunks

1 tsp sugar

½ tsp fish sauce

Salt and pepper to taste

½ cup roasted cashews

1 tbsp lime juice

Salt and pepper to taste

Small bunch of cilantro, chopped for garnish

Cooking Instructions

Sauté the onion and carrots in the olive oil in a large stockpot set over medium heat until fragrant, about 5 minutes. Add the garlic, salt, curry paste, ginger and white pepper. Cook for 2 minutes, stirring constantly. Add the chicken, bay leaves, coconut milk and stock to the pot, bring to a simmer and cook for 10 minutes. Add the potatoes, sugar and fish sauce. Cook until the potatoes are tender, about 15 minutes. Check the chicken to make sure it's cooked through and if not, cook for another 7 to 10 minutes. Taste the soup and adjust seasonings as necessary with salt and pepper. Remove from the heat and stir in the lime juice and cashews. Garnish with fresh cilantro.

Chef's Note:

This stew is jampacked with flavor while being more mild than most other Thai curries.

Serves 4-6 | PREP TIME: 10 minutes. COOK TIME: 30 minutes.

SPICY AFRICAN FISH STEW

This is our take on a traditional African fish stew that's flavorful and simple to prepare. The combination of the spicy harissa and sweet apricot makes this dish unique. Try serving it over couscous with a cold glass of Viognier. Picturesque sunset optional.

Ingredients

1 medium onion, diced

1 large green pepper, diced

2 tbsp olive oil

3 cloves garlic, minced

2 tbsp tomato paste

½ tsp salt

½ tsp cumin

½ tsp turmeric

2 tsp harissa*

3 fresh tomatoes, diced (or one 14.5 ounce canned diced tomatoes)

32 oz fish stock

1 medium potato, peeled and diced

4 oz dried apricots, diced

Pinch of saffron threads

1 lb firm fish filets, such as perch, catfish or walleye, boned and cut into 1 inch pieces

Salt and pepper to taste

Cooking Instructions

Sauté the onion and green pepper in the olive oil in a large stockpot set over medium heat until fragrant, about 5 minutes. Add the garlic, tomato paste, spices (except saffron) and harissa, and cook for 2 minutes, stirring constantly. Add the tomatoes and stock to the pot, and bring to a simmer. Add the potato, apricots and saffron. Cover, turn heat to low and cook until the potatoes are just tender, about 20 minutes. Add the fish and cook uncovered for another 10-12 minutes, just until the fish is cooked through. Taste the soup and adjust seasonings as necessary with salt and pepper.

Serves 4-6 | PREP TIME: 15 minutes. COOK TIME: 45 minutes.

WEST AFRICAN PEANUT STEW

Spicy, salty, and sweet all at the same time, this unusual and delicious stew is sure to please. And the ingredients are easy to find! Serve this with rice or fresh rolls on the side.

Ingredients

1 medium onion, diced

1 carrot, diced

1 tbsp olive oil

3 cloves garlic, minced

½ tsp salt

1 tbsp tomato paste

1 1-inch piece of ginger, peeled and diced

½ tsp crushed red chili flakes, or less to taste

½ tsp ground coriander

¼ tsp white pepper

1 lb boneless skinless chicken breast, cut into chunks

32 oz chicken stock

2 large sweet potatoes, peeled and cut into chunks

½ cup peanut butter

1 tsp cider vinegar

½ cup roasted peanuts

GLUTEN FREE

Cooking Instructions

Sauté the onion and carrots in the olive oil in a large stockpot set over medium heat until fragrant, about 5 minutes. Add the garlic, salt, tomato paste, ginger, chili flakes, coriander and white pepper. Cook for 2 minutes more, stirring constantly. Add the chicken and stock, bring to a simmer and cook for 10 minutes. Add the sweet potatoes, peanut butter, vinegar and peanuts. Cook until the sweet potatoes are tender, about 15 minutes. Check the chicken and make sure it's cooked through, otherwise cook for another 7 to 10 minutes. Taste the soup and adjust seasonings as necessary with salt and pepper. Garnish with fresh scallions and serve.

Chef's Note:

You can serve this dish with tea bread, if you can find it.
Similar to a common French loaf or baguette,
it's a bit more dense and slightly sweet.

Serves 4-6 | PREP TIME: 10 minutes. COOK TIME: 35 minutes.

CHICKEN FAJITA STEW

Ingredients

1 large red onion, chopped

2 poblano peppers, chopped

2 red peppers, chopped

2 tbsp olive oil

3 cloves garlic, minced

1 tsp salt

1 tsp black pepper

2 tsp cumin

1 tbsp chili powder

1 tsp oregano

32 oz chicken stock

2 medium tomatoes, chopped

1 lb chicken, cubed

1 cup red beans, soaked overnight

1 cup rice

1 tbsp hot sauce

4 tbsp fresh cilantro, chopped

Salt and pepper to taste

1 cup queso fresco, crumbled for garnish

Note: You'll need to soak the beans overnight.

Cooking Instructions

Sauté the onions and peppers in the olive oil in a large stockpot set over medium heat until the onions are translucent, about 7-10 minutes. Add the garlic, salt, pepper, cumin, chili powder and oregano. Cook for one minute, stirring constantly. Add the stock and tomatoes, and bring to a simmer. Add the chicken and beans. Cover and cook for 20 minutes to allow the flavors to develop and beans to soften. Add the rice and cook, uncovered, until the chicken and rice are done, and the beans are tender, about 20 minutes longer. Remove the pot from the heat and stir in the hot sauce and 2 tablespoons of the fresh cilantro. Taste the stew and adjust seasonings with salt and pepper as needed.

Ladle stew into 6 bowls. Garnish with the queso fresco and the remaining cilantro.

GLUTEN FREE

Serves 6 | PREP TIME: 15 minutes. COOK TIME: 50 minutes.

ALAMO RED, PURE TEXAS BEEF CHILI

This recipe is chili in its pure Texas form; no beans, no tomatoes, no filler; just simple beef slow cooked with plenty of seasonings. This chili is perfect in a bowl garnished with a bit of sour cream, lime wedges, and a slice of jalapeño, cheddar corn bread. This is also my go-to recipe for topping nachos and chili dogs.

Ingredients

2 lbs boneless beef chuck roast, trimmed and cut into ½ inch cubes

3 tbsp canola oil

4 cloves garlic, minced

1 tsp salt

6 tbsp chili powder

1 tbsp cumin

2 tsp onion powder

2 tsp oregano

1 tsp cayenne pepper

32 oz beef stock

4 tbsp flour

Cooking Instructions

Brown the beef in the canola oil over medium heat in a large stockpot or Dutch oven, about 8 minutes. Add the garlic, salt, 4 tablespoons of the chili powder and the rest of the spices. Cook for 1 minute, stirring constantly. Add half the beef stock and bring to a slow simmer. Cook uncovered for 30 minutes to allow the flavors to develop, stirring often to keep the beef from scorching. Mix the flour with the remaining 2 tablespoons of chili powder and add to the pot. Stir well for 3 minutes. Add the other half of the beef stock. Return to a slow simmer and cook, uncovered, for one more hour (or more until the chili is as thick as you prefer) stirring often to prevent scorching.

Chef's Note:

You can throw the chuck roast in the freezer for 45 minutes or so prior to cooking. This takes it to a firm state that's a lot easier to cut, and small ¼ inch cubes are best for this recipe.

Serves 6 | PREP TIME: 10 minutes. COOK TIME: 90 minutes.

CHAPTER SEVEN

LIGHT, WARM-WEATHER SOUPS

When most people think of soup, they think of something hot and steamy to help keep them warm in a blistering winter night. Or they think of soup as something they eat when they are sick to help them get better. However, soup can take many different forms and doesn't always have to be a winter dish or something you eat when you're sick.

Soup is a year-round meal and is generally very versatile, so it should come to little surprise that it is also a popular summer dish. They can be cold. Gazpacho (a Spanish soup) is a great example of a popular cold soup. Soups can also be desserts. Soup offers anything and everything. Whether you want something big and hearty, or light and elegant, soup is your friend.

In this chapter, you'll be able to experience a couple of distinctive cold soups that will have you eating soup even in the hottest month of the year. As said above, soup is your friend, let it accompany you through the months. Your taste buds will thank you.

GAZPACHO SOUP

Gazpacho is a cold soup originated in Spain that is popular worldwide. This version of gazpacho starts with the traditional tomato base, is thickened with a little bread and comes alive with fresh garlic, red wine vinegar, and savory cumin.

Ingredients

2 slices stale bread, crusts removed

1 cup tomato juice

4 large tomatoes, peeled, seeded and chopped*

1 large cucumber, peeled, seeded and chopped

1 medium red onion, chopped

1 red pepper, diced

2 cloves garlic, minced

½ tsp salt

¼ tsp cumin

¼ tsp cayenne

2 tbsp red wine vinegar

2 tsp clover honey

Salt and cayenne pepper to taste

2 tbsp extra-virgin olive oil

1 to 2 cups cold water as needed

Fresh parsley, chopped for garnish

Note: You'll need some dry, stale bread for this recipe to absorb and thicken the soup, while adding a delicious tangy flavor. You can also put some bread in the oven at 350 degrees for 30 minutes so it is dried through.

Cooking Instructions

Soak the bread slices in the tomato juice. Place the tomatoes, cucumber, onion and bread slices with tomato juice in a blender and purée until smooth. Pour out into a large bowl and add the red pepper, garlic, salt, cumin, cayenne, vinegar and honey. Cover the bowl and put it into the refrigerator for at least one hour and up to overnight. Remove from the refrigerator and adjust seasonings as necessary with salt and a little more cayenne, if needed. Drizzle in the extra-virgin olive oil. Add water if the soup is too thick. It should be smooth and thick but level in the bowl and pourable. Ladle the soup into serving bowls and then top with fresh parsley.

* Here's a friendly reminder on how to peel tomatoes in case you missed it before-Cut a cross on the bottom with a sharp knife and dunk them in boiling water for a minute, then dunk them in cold water. The skin should easily peel back.

Serves 4-6 | PREP TIME: 25 minutes. COOK TIME: Marinate for an hour and up to overnight in the refrigerator.

COOL CUCUMBER SOUP WITH MINT

This an easy recipe for a hot day.

Ingredients

3 large cucumbers, peeled, seeds removed and cut into rough chunks

2 cups plain yogurt

2 tsp lemon juice

½ tsp salt

¼ tsp dried tarragon

¼ tsp granulated garlic

¼ tsp freshly ground black pepper

3 scallions, two chopped, one thinly sliced (the latter is not going into the blender)

Fresh mint leaves, chopped for garnish

Cooking Instructions

Put all the ingredients save the mint leaves and sliced scallion into a blender and purée until smooth. Pour out into a large bowl, add the mint and scallion, and refrigerate for two hours. Remove and adjust seasonings as necessary with salt and pepper. Ladle into bowls and garnish with mint leaves.

Chef's Note:

One of the easiest and quickest soups to make (not counting chill time), this is great to serve as a first course before a larger savory entrée.

Serves 6 | PREP TIME: 25 minutes. COOK TIME: 2 hours in the refrigerator.

CHILLED TOMATO & AVOCADO SOUP

This smooth and flavorful soup is the perfect first-course accompaniment to anything you might be putting on the grill on a beautiful summers night.

Ingredients

4 large tomatoes, peeled, seeded and chopped
1 cucumber, peeled, seeded and chopped
1 ½ cups tomato juice
1 small Vidalia onion, diced
1 clove garlic, minced
½ tsp salt
¼ tsp oregano
¼ tsp freshly ground black pepper
3 avocados, pitted
1 tbsp lime juice
2 scallions, thinly sliced
1 jalapeño, seeded and diced
Pinch of salt
2 tsp extra virgin olive oil for garnish

Cooking Instructions

Place the tomatoes, cucumber and tomato juice in a blender and purée until smooth. Pour out into a large bowl and add the onion, garlic, salt, oregano and black pepper. Mash two of the avocados and stir into the soup. Cover the bowl and put it into the refrigerator for at least one hour and up to four. Dice the third avocado and put it in another bowl, and add the lime juice, scallions, jalapeño and a pinch of salt. Mix well. Ladle the soup into bowls and top with the diced avocados and scallions. Garnish with a drizzle of the extra-virgin olive oil.

Chef's Note:

This soup is perfect to serve with some salty ham and several glasses of sangria.

Serves 4 | PREP TIME: 25 minutes. COOK TIME: Refrigerate for a minimum of 1 hour and up to 4 hours.

CHILLED MELON SOUP

This unique and delicious change-of-pace soup that stands equally well as a first or last course. You can eat this soup in the heat of summer with open-faced sandwiches and some sweet tea for lunch.

Ingredients

1 medium and ripe cantaloupe, peeled, seeded and cut into chunks

1 medium and ripe honeydew, peeled, seeded and cut into chunks

1 large cucumber, peeled, seeded and cut into chunks

1 cup orange juice

1 tbsp honey

¼ tsp salt

¼ tsp ground ginger

Pinch cayenne pepper (be careful to not rub your eyes)

1 cup plain yogurt

Fresh mint leaves

Cooking Instructions

Put the melon, cucumber and orange juice into a blender, and purée until smooth. Pour out into a large bowl and add the honey, salt, ginger and cayenne. Mix well with a whisk to combine. Put the soup into the refrigerator for one hour. Remove and ladle into bowls. Garnish with a dollop of yogurt and a few mint leaves.

Chef's Note:

Some people prefer to blend the yogurt into the soup, but you can also add it at the end for presentation if you prefer instead. You can use this exact recipe (minus the yogurt and cayenne) to make popsicles.

Serves 6 | PREP TIME: 20 minutes. COOK TIME: 1 hour in the refrigerator.

TOMATO VEGETABLE SOUP

It's quick and tasty, and can be frozen to save a taste of summer for the colder months.

Ingredients

1 medium onion, diced

2 carrots, sliced

2 stalks celery, diced

1 tbsp butter

1 tbsp olive oil

½ tsp salt

4 cloves garlic, minced

2 tbsp tomato paste

½ tsp thyme

¼ tsp white pepper

2 lbs fresh tomatoes, blanched, peeled and chopped

32 oz vegetable stock

1 cup orzo pasta

1 zucchini, sliced

1 yellow squash, sliced

Salt and pepper to taste

Cooking Instructions

Sauté the onion, carrots and celery in the butter and olive oil in a large stockpot set over medium heat until fragrant, about 5 minutes. Add the salt, garlic, tomato paste, thyme and white pepper, and cook for two minutes, stirring constantly. Add the tomatoes and their juice as well as the vegetable stock, and bring to a simmer. Add the orzo, zucchini and yellow squash. Cook until the orzo is tender, about 10-12 minutes. Taste the soup and adjust seasonings as necessary with salt and pepper.

Chef's Note:

If you don't have orzo pasta, feel free to substitute long grain rice.

Serves 6-8 | PREP TIME: 10 minutes. COOK TIME: 25 minutes.

COLD ENGLISH PEA & WATERCRESS SOUP WITH MINT

Elegant and nourishing, this easy-to-make chilled soup is a perfect first course for a summer's eve dinner party. Paired with half a roasted turkey club sandwich, it makes a knockout lunch as well.

Ingredients

2 shallots, chopped

2 tbsp butter

1 garlic clove, chopped

1 tsp salt

¼ tsp white pepper

32 oz chicken stock

2 medium Yukon gold potatoes, peeled and quartered

3 cups fresh shelled English peas

1 cup packed fresh watercress, washed and chopped

Salt and pepper to taste

2 tbsp mint leaves

creme fraiche to garnish

Cooking Instructions

Sauté the shallots in the butter in a large stockpot over medium heat until fragrant, about 5 minutes. Add the garlic, salt and pepper. Cook for 1 minute, stirring constantly. Add the stock and bring the soup to a rapid simmer. Add the potatoes and cook for 10 minutes until tender. Add the peas and cook for 3 minutes. Remove from the heat and add the watercress. Taste the soup and adjust seasonings as necessary with salt and pepper. Allow the soup to cool and then add one tbsp of the mint and process to a smooth consistency in a food processor, blender or with an immersion blender. Transfer to another container and chill in the refrigerator at least 4 hours or overnight. Ladle the soup into bowls, top with a dollop of crème fraiche and sprinkle with mint leaves.

Serves 6 | PREP TIME: 10 minutes. COOK TIME: 15 minutes plus at least four hours in the refrigerator to chill.

CHAPTER EIGHT

A WORD ON STOCK

Stock is the base foundation for soups. You can make your stock as flavorful as you want it to be, but keep in mind, that you want to add the best ingredients to make the soup as tasty as you imagine it will be. Every stock deserves all your tender, love, and care, so you and your guests can have a great time eating your dish. Stock is painless to prepare.

Though stock is simple to make, it's important to note that you should take your time and follow each step precisely to achieve the best results. Once you've made a stock or three, you'll be amazed at the quality and taste a homemade broth adds to your recipes. You'll never buy canned or powdered bouillon again!

In this chapter, you will have access to a few basic stocks to start making your beloved dishes at home. Whether you're having a solo meal, a small get together, or a big party, you'll be able to make your stock the star of the show. You'll be ready to take on any (or most) soups when you find your special stock broth. Happy Cooking!

BASIC VEGETABLE STOCK

It's possible to get a nicely flavored vegetable stock
if you give the vegetables some time and attention.

Ingredients

2 medium onions, diced
2 carrots, diced
2 stalks celery, diced
1 large tomato, chopped
1 tbsp canola oil
2 cloves garlic, minced
4 oz button mushrooms, diced
2 tbsp tomato paste
½ tsp salt
½ tsp black pepper
½ tsp thyme
½ tsp parsley
1 bay leaf
1 quart cold water

Cooking Instructions

Add the canola oil to a large stockpot and warm over medium heat. When the oil is hot, add the onions, carrots and celery, and cook for 5 minutes. Add the garlic, mushrooms, tomato paste and seasonings. Cook for one minute, stirring constantly. Add the tomatoes and cold water. Bring the stock to a simmer and cook uncovered for 45 minutes to allow the flavors to develop. The stock is then ready to be put through a cheesecloth-lined strainer and transferred to other containers to be refrigerated or frozen.

Makes about 1 quart stock. PREP TIME: 15 minutes. COOK TIME: 1 hour.

BASIC BEEF STOCK

Ingredients

4 lbs beef bones
2 tbsp canola oil
2 large onions, chopped
2 carrots, chopped
2 stalks celery, chopped
2 cloves garlic, smashed
2 cups red wine
1 tsp salt
1 tsp black pepper
1 tsp dried thyme
1 tsp dried parsley
2 bay leaves
2 quarts cold water

Cooking Instructions

Preheat oven to 400 degrees. Put the bones and vegetables into a large bowl and drizzle with the canola oil. Place the bones and vegetables in a large high sided roasting pan. Roast in the oven for 45 minutes. Remove bones from oven and add the red wine. Let the roasting pan sit for 15 minutes. Remove the bones and vegetables from the roasting pan and add them to a stockpot. Use a spatula to scrape the roasting pan, getting all the browned bits off the bottom and add all that to the stockpot. Add the cold water and spices, and bring the stock to a simmer. Continue cooking until reduced by half, about 2-3 hours, skimming off any foam or scum that rises to the surface. Strain and transfer to other containers and refrigerate or freeze.

Chef's Note:

This stock can be easily defatted; simply skim the stock after it has spent a night in the fridge.

Makes about 1 quart stock. PREP TIME: 15 minutes. COOK TIME: 4 hours.

BASIC CHICKEN STOCK

Ingredients

4 lbs chicken backs, necks and wingtips
2 tbsp canola oil
2 large onions, chopped
2 carrots, chopped
2 stalks celery, chopped
2 cloves garlic, smashed
1 tsp salt
1 tsp black pepper
1 tsp dried thyme
1 tsp dried parsley
2 bay leaves
2 cups white wine
2 quarts cold water

Cooking Instructions

Warm the canola oil in a large stockpot over medium heat. Add the onion, carrot and celery, and cook for 5 minutes. Add the garlic and seasonings. Cook for one minute, stirring constantly. Add the chicken parts and cook for 5 minutes more. Add the wine and scrape the bottom of the pan with a spatula to get all the brown bits. Add the cold water and bring the stock to a simmer. Continue cooking until reduced by half, about 2-3 hours, being sure to skim any foam or scum that rises to the surface. After the stock has been reduced, it is ready to be put through a strainer and transferred to other containers to be refrigerated or frozen.

Chef's Note:

Like the beef stock, this stock can be easily defatted by skimming the stock after it has spent a night in the fridge.

Makes about 1 quart stock. PREP TIME: 15 minutes. COOK TIME: 4 hours.

BASIC FISH STOCK

Fish stock is slightly different from beef or chicken stock, namely it takes far less time.

Ingredients

2 lbs fish bones and/or heads (we use both)
1 large onion, chopped
1 carrot, chopped
1 stalk celery, chopped
1 clove garlic, smashed
½ tsp salt
½ tsp black pepper
½ tsp dried thyme
½ tsp dried parsley
1 bay leaf
1 cup white wine
1 quart cold water
1 tbsp canola oil

Cooking Instructions

Add the canola oil to a large stockpot and warm over medium heat. Add the onion, carrot and celery and cook for 5 minutes. Add the garlic and the seasonings and cook for one minute, stirring constantly. Add the fish bones and heads, and cook for 5 minutes more. Add the wine and scrape the bottom of the pan with a spatula to get all the brown bits. Add the cold water and bring the stock to a simmer. Cook uncovered for 30 minutes to allow the flavors to develop, being sure to skim any foam or scum that rises to the surface. Do not overcook or the stock will be bitter. After 30 minutes have passed the stock is ready to be put through a fine strainer and transferred to other containers to be refrigerated or frozen. Be sure to use a very fine mesh strainer or line your strainer with a cheesecloth to keep the broth nice and clear.

Makes about 1 quart stock. | PREP TIME. 15 minutes. COOK TIME. 1 hour.

ABOUT THE AUTHORS

Garland Dru Melton has been in the restaurant industry his whole life and started working in the kitchen at a young age with his grandmother and mother, a restaurant industry veteran. He went on to cooking school and has taken his cooking influence equally from top Chicago chefs as well as his small-town, farm upbringing in Chillicothe, IL that emphasized fresh, wholesome, and locally produced ingredients. He has over 25 years of restaurant experience and been everything from a busboy to head chef. He is now the general manager of the Soupbox.

Jamie Taerbaum started his restaurant, the Soupbox in 1995 on a shoestring and has grown it into the most popular and best reviewed soup restaurant in Chicago. It has been featured in practically every major network and newspaper in Chicago, including a recommendation from ABC's "Hungry Hound."

ACKNOWLEDGMENTS

Jamie: I'd like to thank my mom for having me and raising five kids on her own. Otherwise there would be no Soupbox. And I would like to extend my appreciation to Dru for his dedication day after day making Soupbox a special place and eliciting thoughts of family, well-being, and comfort.

Dru: To Christine, Pearl, Max, and the rest of my family. Thank you for all the love and support you provide. To Jamie for keeping a hand on the wheel and letting me run with the ball. To my editor Will, who has made this entire process a joy.

RECIPE INDEX

A

Abalone Soup with Straw Mushrooms, Ginger & Rice Noodles, 172

Alamo Red, Pure Texas Beef Chili, 209

Alaskan King Crab & Sweet Corn Chowder, 154

Albondigas or Mexican Meatball Soup, 75

Asian Pork & Glass Noodle Soup, 79

Avocado & Artichoke Bisque, 141

B

Bacon, Tomato & Cheddar Chowder, 67

Basic Beef Stock, 229

Basic Chicken Stock, 230

Basic Fish Stock, 231

Basic Vegetable Stock, 228

Bayou Chicken & Sausage Gumbo, 68

Beef Borscht, 76

Beer & Cheese with Smoked Bacon Soup, 131

Big Occasion Bouillabaisse, 161

Birthday Soup, 44

Broccoli Rabe Soup with Lentils & Spring Onions, 57

Broccoli & White Cheddar Soup, 128

Brunswick Stew, 180

C

Cabbage & Smoked Sausage Stew, 181

Cajun Crawfish Chowder, 158

California Vegetable Medley Soup, 22

Cantonese Chicken Chowder, 109

Caribbean Jerk Chicken Chowder, 110

Chicken Azteca, 105

Chicken Fajita Stew, 208

Chickpea Chowder with Purslane & Leeks, 129

Chilled Melon Soup, 221

Chilled Tomato & Avocado Soup, 218

Chipotle Sweet Potato Bisque, 133

Chorizo & Sweet-Potato Stew, 182

Cioppino Soup, 148

Classic Chicken Noodle Soup, 99

Classic She-Crab Soup, 165

Cock-a-leekie Stew, 184

Cold English Pea & Watercress Soup with Mint, 223

Colorado Green Chili, 190

Cool Cucumber Soup with Mint, 217

Cream of Potato & Leek Soup, 135

Cream of Spinach with Roasted Garlic Soup, 143

Creamy Chicken & Wild Rice Soup, 92

Creole Shrimp Bisque, 159

Cuban Black Bean Soup, 30

Curried Shrimp Soup with Mango, 162

D

Deep South Burgoo, 198

Delicious Farro & Cannellini Bean Stew, 189

The Divine Cream of Mushroom Soup, 132

Duck Soup, 121

F

Fire-Roasted Vegetable Soup, 18

Fresh Tomato & Basil Bisque, 51

G

Gazpacho Soup, 214

Greek Avgolemono Soup, 117

Green Bean & Zucchini Soup with Quinoa, 58

H

Healthy Halibut Chowder, 157

Heart-Healthy Vegetarian Chili, 193

Hearty Beef Stew, 179

Hearty Fresh Vegetable, 21

Hot & Sour Soup (Tom Yum), 167

I

Indonesian Crab Soup with Lemongrass, 164

Israeli Eggplant Stew with Couscous, 199

Italian Wedding Soup, 71

L

Lentil Soup with Lemon, 41

Lobster Bisque, 126

M

Maryland Crab Chowder, 153

Masala Tomato Lentil, 42

Massaman Chicken Curry Stew, 204

Mediterranean Vegetable Soup, 25

Mexican Tortilla Soup, 106

Mulligatawny Soup, 55

Mushroom Barley Soup, 16

N

Nantucket Oyster Stew, 149

New England Clam Chowder, 150

North African Vegetable Soup, 26

O

Old West Chicken Adobo, 108

P

Persian Lamb & Spinach Stew, 201

Pizza Lovers' Soup, 72

Poblano Chicken Chili, 195

Pure Texas Beef Chili, 209

R

Red Bean Chicken Chili, 187

Roadhouse Beef Chili, 192

Roasted Butternut Squash Soup with Sage and Apple, 15

Roasted Carrot & Fennel Soup, 43

Roasted Carrot & Ginger Bisque, 47

Roasted Chicken Florentine, 96

Roasted Chicken Pot Pie Soup, 98

Roasted Chicken with Pesto & Pink Lentils, 118

Roasted Corn & Green Chili Chowder, 136

Roasted Garlic Scape Bisque, 137

Roasted Tomato & Red Pepper Bisque, 138

Roasted Turkey with Egg Noodle Soup, 113

Rosemary Chicken Dumpling Soup, 95

Rouille, 161

Rustic Cauliflower & Cabbage Chowder, 140

S

Sausage & Barley Soup, 86

Savory Cream of Asparagus, 48

Seven-Bean Mélange, 19

Shrimp Soba Noodle Soup, 171

Sichuan Beef Noodle Soup, 73

Sicilian Chicken Soup with Bowtie Pasta, 103

Slow Cooker Jambalaya, 202

Smoked Ham with Great Northern White Beans, 64

Smoked Salmon Stew, 185

Southern Comfort Soup with Smoked Bacon & Collard Greens, 87

Spicy African Fish Stew, 205

Spicy Beef with Ramen Noodle Soup, 82

Spicy Lentil & Lamb Sausage Stew, 66

Spicy Mayan Chicken Enchilada, 104

Spicy Southwestern White Bean Soup, 32

Split-Pea Soup, 37

Stuffed Green Pepper Soup, 56

Sunchoke Bisque with Roasted Sweet Peppers, 142

Sun-Dried Tomato & Roasted Garlic Soup, 52

Sweet Corn Chowder, 29

Sweet & Sour Fish Stew, 168

T

Taco Soup, 84

Tasmanian Duck Soup, 119

Tex-Mex Turkey & Tomato Soup, 115

Thai Coconut Shrimp Curry, 188

Tomato Florentine Soup, 53

Tomato Vegetable Soup, 222

Tortellini Con Brodo, 100

Tunisian Fish Chowder, 173

Turkey Soup with Chorizo, Potatoes & Leeks, 120

Turkey & Wild Mushroom Soup, 114

V

Vegetable Soup, 59

Vietnamese Pho with Beef, 80

W

West African Peanut Stew, 207

West Indian Squash Sambar, 33

White Bean & Escarole Soup, 34

White Bean Turkey Chili, 196

Y

Yellow Split-Pea Soup with Fennel, 38

INDEX

Abalone Soup with Straw Mushrooms, Ginger & Rice Noodles, 172
acini di pepe pasta
   Fire Roasted Vegetable Soup, 18
   Italian Wedding Soup, 71
Alamo Red, Pure Texas Beef Chili, 209
Alaskan King Crab & Sweet Corn Chowder, 154
Albondigas or Mexican Meatball Soup, 75
Andouille sausage
   Bayou Chicken & Sausage Gumbo, 68
   Brunswick Stew, 180
   Slow Cooker Jambalaya, 202
apples
   Hearty Beef Stew, 179
   Mulligatawny Soup, 55
   Roasted Butternut Squash Soup with Sage and Apple, 15
   Tasmanian Duck Soup, 119
artichokes
   Avocado & Artichoke Bisque, 141
   Mediterranean Vegetable Soup, 25
   Sunchoke Bisque with Roasted Sweet Peppers, 142
Asian Pork & Glass Noodle Soup, 79
avocados
   Avocado & Artichoke Bisque, 141
   Chilled Tomato & Avocado Soup, 218
   Poblano Chicken Chili, 195

bacon
   Bacon, Tomato & Cheddar Chowder, 67
   Beer & Cheese with Smoked Bacon Soup, 131
   Cajun Crawfish Chowder, 158
   Green Bean & Zucchini Soup with Quinoa, 58
   Smoked Salmon Stew, 185
   Southern Comfort Soup with Smoked Bacon & Collard Greens, 87
   Sweet Corn Chowder, 29
   White Bean & Escarole Soup, 34
barley
   Cock-a-leekie Stew, 184
   Duck Soup, 121
   Mushroom Barley Soup, 16
   Sausage & Barley Soup, 86
Basic Beef Stock, 229
Basic Chicken Stock, 230
Basic Fish Stock, 231
Basic Vegetable Stock, 228
Bayou Chicken & Sausage Gumbo, 68
beans
   Broccoli Rabe Soup with Lentils & Spring Onions, 57
   Brunswick Stew, 180
   Chicken Fajita Stew, 208
   Colorado Green Chili, 190
   Cuban Black Bean Soup, 30
   Delicious Farro & Cannellini Bean Stew, 189
   Heart Healthy Vegetarian Chili, 193

Lentil Soup with Lemon, 41
Masala Tomato Lentil, 42
Mexican Tortilla Soup, 106
Mulligatawny Soup, 55
Poblano Chicken Chili, 195
Red Bean Chicken Chili, 187
Roadhouse Beef Chili, 192
Seven Bean Mélange, 19
Smoked Ham with Great Northern White Beans, 64
Spicy Lentil & Lamb Sausage Stew, 66
Spicy Mayan Chicken Enchilada, 104
Spicy Southwestern White Bean Soup, 32
Taco Soup, 84
White Bean & Escarole Soup, 34
White Bean Turkey Chili, 196
beef
   Alamo Red, Pure Texas Beef Chili, 209
   Albondigas or Mexican Meatball Soup, 75
   Basic Beef Stock, 229
   Beef Borscht, 76
   Deep South Burgoo, 198
   Hearty Beef Stew, 179
   Italian Wedding Soup, 71
   Roadhouse Beef Chili, 192
   Sichuan Beef Noodle Soup, 73
   Spicy Beef with Ramen Noodle Soup, 82
   Stuffed Green Pepper Soup, 56
   Taco Soup, 84
   Vietnamese Pho with Beef, 80
beef stock
   Alamo Red, Pure Texas Beef Chili, 209
   Basic Beef Stock, 229
   Deep South Burgoo, 198
   Hearty Beef Stew, 179
   Pizza Lovers' Soup, 72
   Roadhouse Beef Chili, 192
   Sausage & Barley Soup, 86
   Sichuan Beef Noodle Soup, 73
   Spicy Beef with Ramen Noodle Soup, 82
   Stuffed Green Pepper Soup, 56
   Tomato Florentine Soup, 53
Beer & Cheese with Smoked Bacon Soup, 131
bell peppers
   California Vegetable Medley Soup, 22
   Sweet Corn Chowder, 29
   Smoked Ham with Great Northern White Beans, 64
Big Occasion Bouillabaisse, 161
Birthday Soup, 44
black beans
   Cuban Black Bean Soup, 30
   Mexican Tortilla Soup, 106
   Spicy Mayan Chicken Enchilada, 104
black-eyed peas

Seven Bean Mélange, 19
Southern Comfort Soup with Smoked Bacon & Collard Greens, 91
bok choy
  Abalone Soup with Straw Mushrooms, Ginger & Rice Noodles, 172
  Sichuan Beef Noodle Soup, 73
  Shrimp Soba Noodle Soup, 171
broccoli
  Broccoli Rabe Soup with Lentils & Spring Onions, 57
  Broccoli & White Cheddar Soup, 128
Brunswick Stew, 180
button mushrooms
  Basic Vegetable Stock, 228
  Divine Cream of Mushroom Soup, 132
  Mushroom Barley Soup, 16
  Turkey & Wild Mushroom Soup, 114

cabbage
  Cabbage & Smoked Sausage Stew, 181
  Deep South Burgoo, 198
  Rustic Cauliflower & Cabbage Chowder, 140
Cajun Crawfish Chowder, 158
California Vegetable Medley Soup, 22
Cannellini beans
  Delicious Farro & Cannellini Bean Stew, 189
  White Bean & Escarole Soup, 34
Cantonese Chicken Chowder, 109
Caribbean Jerk Chicken Chowder, 110
carrots
  Abalone Soup with Straw Mushrooms, Ginger & Rice Noodles, 172
  Alaskan King Crab & Sweet Corn Chowder, 154
  Albondigas or Mexican Meatball Soup, 75
  Asian Pork & Glass Noodle Soup, 79
  Avocado & Artichoke Bisque, 141
  Beef Borscht, 76
  Birthday Soup, 44
  Bacon, Tomato & Cheddar Chowder, 67
  Basic Beef Stock, 229
  Basic Chicken Stock, 230
  Basic Fish Stock, 231
  Basic Vegetable Stock, 228
  Beer & Cheese with Smoked Bacon Soup, 131
  Broccoli Rabe Soup with Lentils & Spring Onions, 57
  Broccoli & White Cheddar Soup, 128
  Cabbage & Smoked Sausage Stew, 181
  California Vegetable Medley Soup, 22
  Cantonese Chicken Chowder, 109
  Caribbean Jerk Chicken Chowder, 110
  Chicken Azteca, 105
  Chickpea Chowder with Purslane & Leeks, 129
  Chipotle Sweet Potato Bisque, 133
  Chorizo & Sweet-Potato Stew, 182
  Cioppino Soup, 148
  Classic Chicken Noodle Soup, 99
  Cock-a-leekie Stew, 184
  Colorado Green Chili, 190
  Cream of Potato & Leek Soup, 135
  Creamy Chicken & Wild Rice Soup, 92
  Cuban Black Bean Soup, 30
  Deep South Burgoo, 198
  Delicious Farro & Cannellini Bean Stew, 189
  Duck Soup, 121

Fire Roasted Vegetable Soup, 18
Fresh Tomato & Basil Bisque, 51
Green Bean & Zucchini Soup with Quinoa, 58
Healthy Halibut Chowder, 157
Heart Healthy Vegetarian Chili, 193
Hearty Beef Stew, 179
Hearty Fresh Vegetable, 21
Indonesian Crab Soup with Lemongrass, 164
Israeli Eggplant Stew with Couscous, 199
Italian Wedding Soup, 71
Lentil Soup with Lemon, 41
Lobster Bisque, 126
Masala Tomato Lentil, 42
Massaman Chicken Curry Stew, 204
Mediterranean Vegetable Soup, 25
Mexican Tortilla Soup, 106
Mulligatawny Soup, 55
Mushroom Barley Soup, 16
Nantucket Oyster Stew, 149
North African Vegetable Soup, 26
Old West Chicken Adobo, 108
Persian Lamb & Spinach Stew, 201
Roasted Butternut Squash Soup with Sage and Apple, 15
Roasted Carrot & Fennel Soup, 43
Roasted Carrot & Ginger Bisque, 47
Roasted Chicken Florentine, 96
Roasted Chicken Pot Pie Soup, 98
Roasted Chicken with Pesto & Pink Lentils, 118
Roasted Corn & Green Chili Chowder, 136
Roasted Garlic Scape Bisque, 137
Roasted Tomato & Red Pepper Bisque, 138
Roasted Turkey with Egg Noodle Soup, 113
Rosemary Chicken Dumpling Soup, 95
Rustic Cauliflower & Cabbage Chowder, 140
Sausage & Barley Soup, 86
Seven Bean Mélange, 19
Sicilian Chicken Soup with Bowtie Pasta, 103
Smoked Ham with Great Northern White Beans, 64
Southern Comfort Soup with Smoked Bacon & Collard Greens, 87
Spicy Beef with Ramen Noodle Soup, 82
Spicy Lentil & Lamb Sausage Stew, 66
Spicy Mayan Chicken Enchilada, 104
Spicy Southwestern White Bean Soup, 32
Split-Pea Soup, 37
Shrimp Soba Noodle Soup, 171
Sun-Dried Tomato & Roasted Garlic Soup, 52
Taco Soup, 84
Tasmanian Duck Soup, 119
Tex Mex Turkey & Tomato Soup, 115
Tomato Florentine Soup, 53
Tomato Vegetable Soup, 222
Tortellini con Brodo, 100
Turkey & Wild Mushroom Soup, 114
Vegetable Soup, 59
West African Peanut Stew, 207
West Indian Squash Sambar, 33
White Bean Turkey Chili, 196
Yellow Split-Pea Soup with Fennel, 38
celery
  Alaskan King Crab & Sweet Corn Chowder, 154
  Albondigas or Mexican Meatball Soup, 75
  Asian Pork & Glass Noodle Soup, 79
  Avocado & Artichoke Bisque, 141

Bacon, Tomato & Cheddar Chowder, 67
Basic Beef Stock, 229
Basic Chicken Stock, 230
Basic Fish Stock, 231
Basic Vegetable Stock, 228
Bayou Chicken & Sausage Gumbo, 68
Beef Borscht, 76
Beer & Cheese with Smoked Bacon Soup, 131
Big Occasion Bouillabaisse, 161
Birthday Soup, 44
Broccoli Rabe Soup with Lentils & Spring Onions, 57
Brunswick Stew, 180
Cabbage & Smoked Sausage Stew, 181
Cajun Crawfish Chowder, 158
California Vegetable Medley Soup, 22
Cantonese Chicken Chowder, 109
Caribbean Jerk Chicken Chowder, 110
Chicken Azteca, 105
Chickpea Chowder with Purslane & Leeks, 129
Chipotle Sweet Potato Bisque, 133
Cioppino Soup, 148
Classic Chicken Noodle Soup, 99
Classic She-Crab Soup, 165
Cock-a-leekie Stew, 184
Colorado Green Chili, 190
Cream of Potato & Leek Soup, 135
Creamy Chicken & Wild Rice Soup, 92
Creole Shrimp Bisque, 159
Curried Shrimp Soup with Mango, 162
Deep South Burgoo, 198
Delicious Farro & Cannellini Bean Stew, 189
Duck Soup, 121
Green Bean & Zucchini Soup with Quinoa, 58
Healthy Halibut Chowder, 157
Heart-Healthy Vegetarian Chili, 193
Hearty Beef Stew, 179
Hearty Fresh Vegetable, 21
Indonesian Crab Soup with Lemongrass, 164
Italian Wedding Soup, 71
Lentil Soup with Lemon, 41
Lobster Bisque, 126
Maryland Crab Chowder, 153
Masala Tomato Lentil, 42
Mexican Tortilla Soup, 106
Mulligatawny Soup, 55
Mushroom Barley Soup, 16
Nantucket Oyster Stew, 149
New England Clam Chowder, 150
Old West Chicken Adobo, 108
Poblano Chicken Chili, 195
Red Bean Chicken Chili, 187
Roadhouse Beef Chili, 192
Roasted Carrot & Fennel Soup, 43
Roasted Chicken Florentine, 96
Roasted Chicken Pot Pie Soup, 98
Roasted Chicken with Pesto & Pink Lentils, 118
Roasted Corn & Green Chili Chowder, 136
Roasted Garlic Scape Bisque, 137
Roasted Turkey with Egg Noodle Soup, 113
Rosemary Chicken Dumpling Soup, 95
Rustic Cauliflower & Cabbage Chowder, 140
Sausage & Barley Soup, 86
Seven Bean Mélange, 19

Sicilian Chicken Soup with Bowtie Pasta, 103
Slow Cooker Jambalaya, 202
Smoked Ham with Great Northern White Beans, 64
Smoked Salmon Stew, 185
Southern Comfort Soup with Smoked Bacon & Collard Greens, 87
Spicy Beef with Ramen Noodle Soup, 82
Spicy Lentil & Lamb Sausage Stew, 66
Spicy Mayan Chicken Enchilada, 104
Spicy Southwestern White Bean Soup, 32
Stuffed Green Pepper Soup, 56
Sun-Dried Tomato & Roasted Garlic Soup, 52
Sweet & Sour Fish Stew, 168
Taco Soup, 84
Tasmanian Duck Soup, 119
Tex Mex Turkey & Tomato Soup, 115
Tomato Florentine Soup, 53
Tomato Vegetable Soup, 222
Tortellini con Brodo, 100
Tunisian Fish Chowder, 173
Turkey & Wild Mushroom Soup, 114
Vegetable Soup, 59
White Bean & Escarole Soup, 34
White Bean Turkey Chili, 196
Yellow Split-Pea Soup with Fennel, 38
cheese
    Bacon, Tomato & Cheddar Chowder, 67
    Beer & Cheese with Smoked Bacon Soup, 131
    Broccoli & White Cheddar Soup, 128
    California Vegetable Medley Soup, 22
    Fresh Tomato & Basil Bisque, 51
    Italian Wedding Soup, 71
    Pizza Lovers' Soup, 72
chicken
    Basic Chicken Stock, 230
    Bayou Chicken & Sausage Gumbo, 68
    Brunswick Stew, 180
    Cantonese Chicken Chowder, 109
    Caribbean Jerk Chicken Chowder, 110
    Chicken Azteca, 105
    Chicken Fajita Stew, 208
    Classic Chicken Noodle Soup, 99
    Cock-a-leekie Stew, 184
    Creamy Chicken & Wild Rice Soup, 92
    Greek Avgolemono Soup, 117
    Israeli Eggplant Stew with Couscous, 199
    Massaman Chicken Curry Stew, 204
    Mexican Tortilla Soup, 106
    Mulligatawny Soup, 55
    Old West Chicken Adobo, 108
    Poblano Chicken Chili, 195
    Red Bean Chicken Chili, 187
    Roasted Chicken Florentine, 96
    Roasted Chicken Pot Pie Soup, 98
    Roasted Chicken with Pesto & Pink Lentils, 118
    Rosemary Chicken Dumpling Soup, 95
    Sicilian Chicken Soup with Bowtie Pasta, 103
    Slow Cooker Jambalaya, 202
    Spicy Mayan Chicken Enchilada, 104
    West African Peanut Stew, 207
chicken stock
    Abalone Soup with Straw Mushrooms, Ginger & Rice Noodles, 172
    Albondigas or Mexican Meatball Soup, 75

Bacon, Tomato & Cheddar Chowder, 67
Basic Chicken Stock, 230
Beer & Cheese with Smoked Bacon Soup, 131
Brunswick Stew, 180
Cabbage & Smoked Sausage Stew, 181
Cantonese Chicken Chowder, 109
Caribbean Jerk Chicken Chowder, 110
Chicken Azteca, 105
Chicken Fajita Stew, 208
Chorizo & Sweet-Potato Stew, 182
Classic Chicken Noodle Soup, 99
Cold English Pea & Watercress Soup with Mint, 223
Colorado Green Chili, 190
Cream of Potato & Leek Soup, 135
Creamy Chicken & Wild Rice Soup, 92
Divine Cream of Mushroom Soup, 132
Duck Soup, 121
Greek Avgolemono Soup, 117
Healthy Halibut Chowder, 157
Hot & Sour Soup (Tom Yum), 167
Israeli Eggplant Stew with Couscous, 199
Italian Wedding Soup, 71
Lobster Bisque, 126
Massaman Chicken Curry Stew, 204
Mexican Tortilla Soup, 106
Mulligatawny Soup, 55
Persian Lamb & Spinach Stew, 201
Poblano Chicken Chili, 195
Red Bean Chicken Chili, 187
Roasted Chicken Florentine, 96
Roasted Chicken Pot Pie Soup, 98
Roasted Garlic Scape Bisque, 137
Roasted Tomato & Red Pepper Bisque, 138
Roasted Turkey with Egg Noodle Soup, 113
Roasted Chicken with Pesto & Pink Lentils, 118
Rosemary Chicken Dumpling Soup, 95
Savory Cream of Asparagus, 48
Sicilian Chicken Soup with Bowtie Pasta, 103
Slow Cooker Jambalaya, 202
Smoked Ham with Great Northern White Beans, 64
Southern Comfort Soup with Smoked Bacon & Collard Greens, 91
Spicy Lentil & Lamb Sausage Soup, 66
Spicy Mayan Chicken Enchilada, 104
Split-Pea Soup, 37
Spring Shrimp Soba Noodle Soup, 171
Sun-Dried Tomato & Roasted Garlic Soup, 52
Tasmanian Duck Soup, 119
Tex Mex Turkey & Tomato Soup, 115
Taco Soup, 84
Tortellini con Brodo, 100
Turkey Soup with Chorizo, Potatoes & Leeks, 120
Turkey & Wild Mushroom Soup, 114
West African Peanut Stew, 207
White Bean & Escarole Soup, 34
White Bean Turkey Chili, 196
chickpeas
    Chickpea Chowder with Purslane & Leeks, 129
    Seven Bean Mélange, 19
Chilled Melon Soup, 221
Chilled Tomato & Avocado Soup, 218
chipotle peppers
    Mexican Tortilla Soup, 106
    Chipotle Sweet Potato Bisque, 133

Heart-Healthy Vegetarian Chili, 193
Old West Chicken Adobo, 108
Tex Mex Turkey & Tomato Soup, 115
chorizo
    Chorizo & Sweet-Potato Stew, 182
    Turkey Soup with Chorizo, Potatoes & Leeks, 120
Cioppino Soup, 148
clams
    Big Occasion Bouillabaisse, 161
    Cioppino Soup, 148
    New England Clam Chowder, 150
Classic Chicken Noodle Soup, 99
Classic She-Crab Soup, 165
Cock-a-leekie Stew, 184
coconut milk
    Massaman Chicken Curry Stew, 204
    Thai Coconut Shrimp Curry, 188
    West Indian Squash Sambar, 33
Cold English Pea & Watercress Soup with Mint, 223
collard greens
    Southern Comfort Soup with Smoked Bacon & Collard Greens, 87
    White Bean & Escarole Soup, 34
Colorado Green Chili, 190
Cook's Notes
    Alamo Red, Pure Texas Beef Chili, 209
    beef stock, defatting, 229
    Beer & Cheese with Smoked Bacon Soup, 131
    Big Occasion Bouillabaisse, 161
    Broccoli & White Cheddar Soup, 128
    Brunswick Stew, 180
    Caribbean Jerk Chicken Chowder, 110
    Chicken Azteca, 105
    chicken stock, defatting, 230
    Chilled Melon Soup, 221
    Chilled Tomato & Avocado Soup, 218
    Chipotle Sweet Potato Bisque, 133
    Cioppino Soup, 148
    chuck roast, cubing, 209
    Colorado Green Chili, 190
    Gazpacho Soup, 214
    Greek Avgolemono Soup, 117
    Classic She-Crab Soup, 165
    colds, soup for, 73
    cooking time, reducing, 113
    Cool Cucumber Soup with Mint, 217
    corn, cutting from cob, 29
    cornstarch, thickening with, 161
    crab roe, 165
    Creole Shrimp Bisque, 159
    Curried Shrimp Soup with Mango, 162
    escarole, substituting, 34
    garlic, roasting, 143
    gumbo types, 68
    harissa, substituting, 26
    Indonesian Crab Soup with Lemongrass, 164
    liquid smoke, 19
    Maryland Crab Chowder, 153
    mascarpone cheese garnish, 47
    Massaman Chicken Curry Stew, 204
    meatballs, packing, 71
    meatballs, tenderness of, 71
    meat, browning, 179
    mushrooms, cooking, 132

mushrooms, reconstituting, 172
Nantucket Oyster Stew, 149
Old West Chicken Adobo, 108
orzo pasta, substituting, 222
oysters, 149
peppers, roasting, 30, 32
Pho shortcuts, 85
Poblano Chicken Chili, 195
potatoes for chowder, 67
potatoes, substituting, 114
purslane, substituting, 129
ramen, comfort of, 82
Roasted Turkey with Egg Noodle Soup, 113
rotini, substituting, 44
salt, 42
"second dump" spices, 192
Sicilian Chicken Soup with Bowtie Pasta, 103
side dishes for Taco Soup, 84
Slow Cooker Jambalaya, 202
slow cookers, 190
soy protein, substituting, 193
spring onions, 57
straining, 138
tea bread, 207
Tex Mex Turkey & Tomato Soup, 115
thickness, adding, 96
tomatoes, peeling, 21
Tortellini con Brodo, 100
cook time
    15 minutes
        Cold English Pea & Watercress Soup with Mint, 223
    20 minutes
        Greek Avgolemono Soup, 117
        Indonesian Crab Soup with Lemongrass, 164
        Mulligatawny Soup, 55
        Old West Chicken Adobo, 108
        Roasted Chicken Florentine, 96
        Spicy Beef with Ramen Noodle Soup, 82
        Tortellini con Brodo, 100
    25 minutes
        Asian Pork & Glass Noodle Soup, 79
        Avocado & Artichoke Bisque, 141
        Bacon, Tomato & Cheddar Chowder, 67
        Broccoli Rabe Soup with Lentils & Spring Onions, 57
        Divine Cream of Mushroom Soup, 132
        Hot & Sour Soup (Tom Yum), 167
        Italian Wedding Soup, 71
        Pizza Lovers' Soup, 72
        Sicilian Chicken Soup with Bowtie Pasta, 103
        Shrimp Soba Noodle Soup, 171
        Tomato Vegetable Soup, 222
        Sweet & Sour Fish Stew, 168
        Taco Soup, 84
        Tex Mex Turkey & Tomato Soup, 115
        Thai Coconut Shrimp Curry, 188
    30 minutes
        Alaskan King Crab & Sweet Corn Chowder, 154
        Cajun Crawfish Chowder, 158
        Cantonese Chicken Chowder, 109
        Cioppino Soup, 148
        Classic Chicken Noodle Soup, 99
        Classic She-Crab Soup, 165
        Cream of Spinach with Roasted Garlic Soup, 143

Curried Shrimp Soup with Mango, 162
Green Bean & Zucchini Soup with Quinoa, 58
Heart-Healthy Vegetarian Chili, 193
Hearty Fresh Vegetable, 21
Lentil Soup with Lemon, 41
Massaman Chicken Curry Stew, 204
Mexican Tortilla Soup, 106
Mushroom Barley Soup, 16
New England Clam Chowder, 150
Sausage & Barley Soup, 86
Savory Cream of Asparagus, 48
Seven Bean Mélange, 19
Slow Cooker Jambalaya, 202
Smoked Salmon Stew, 185
Sunchoke Bisque with Roasted Sweet Peppers, 142
Tasmanian Duck Soup, 119
Tunisian Fish Chowder, 173
Turkey Soup with Chorizo, Potatoes & Leeks, 120
West African Peanut Stew, 207
White Bean & Escarole Soup, 34
35 minutes
    Birthday Soup, 44
    Cabbage & Smoked Sausage Stew, 181
    California Vegetable Medley Soup, 22
    Cream of Potato & Leek Soup, 135
    Creole Shrimp Bisque, 159
    Healthy Halibut Chowder, 157
    Lobster Bisque, 130
    Maryland Crab Chowder, 153
    Mediterranean Vegetable Soup, 25
    Nantucket Oyster Stew, 149
    Roasted Carrot & Ginger Bisque, 47
    Roasted Garlic Scape Bisque, 137
    Stuffed Green Pepper Soup, 56
    Sweet Corn Chowder, 29
40 minutes
    Beer & Cheese with Smoked Bacon Soup, 131
    North African Vegetable Soup, 26
    Rosemary Chicken Dumpling Soup, 95
40 to 45 minutes
    Broccoli & White Cheddar Soup, 128
    Fresh Tomato & Basil Bisque, 51
    West Indian Squash Sambar, 33
45 minutes
    Chickpea Chowder with Purslane & Leeks, 129
    Chipotle Sweet Potato Bisque, 133
    Chorizo & Sweet-Potato Stew, 182
    Creamy Chicken & Wild Rice Soup, 92
    Cuban Black Bean Soup, 30
    Duck Soup, 121
    Fire Roasted Vegetable Soup, 18
    Israeli Eggplant Stew with Couscous, 199
    Roasted Carrot & Fennel Soup, 43
    Roasted Corn & Green Chili Chowder, 136
    Roasted Turkey with Egg Noodle Soup, 113
    Rustic Cauliflower & Cabbage Chowder, 140
    Spicy African Fish Stew, 205
    Spicy Lentil & Lamb Sausage Stew, 66
    Spicy Mayan Chicken Enchilada, 104
    Spicy Southwestern White Bean Soup, 32
    Tomato Florentine Soup, 53
    Turkey & Wild Mushroom Soup, 114
    Vegetable Soup, 59

White Bean Turkey Chili, 196
Yellow Split-Pea Soup with Fennel, 38
50 minutes
Chicken Fajita Stew, 208
Delicious Farro & Cannellini Bean Stew, 189
Roasted Tomato & Red Pepper Bisque, 138
Sun-Dried Tomato & Roasted Garlic Soup, 52
1 hour
Basic Beef Stock, 229
Basic Fish Stock, 231
Basic Vegetable Stock, 228
Big Occasion Bouillabaisse, 161
Brunswick Stew, 180
Caribbean Jerk Chicken Chowder, 110
Chicken Azteca, 105
Chilled Melon Soup, 221
Chilled Tomato & Avocado Soup, 218
Cock-a-leekie Stew, 184
Colorado Green Chili, 190
Gazpacho Soup, 214
Persian Lamb & Spinach Stew, 201
Poblano Chicken Chili, 195
Red Bean Chicken Chili, 187
Southern Comfort Soup with Smoked Bacon & Collard Greens,
91
1 hour and 15 minutes
Roasted Chicken Pot Pie Soup, 98
Smoked Ham with Great Northern White Beans, 64
1 hour and 30 minutes
Abalone Soup with Straw Mushrooms, Ginger & Rice Noodles,
172
Alamo Red, Pure Texas Beef Chili, 209
Beef Borscht, 76
Roadhouse Beef Chili, 192
Roasted Butternut Squash Soup with Sage and Apple, 15
Split-Pea Soup, 37
1 hour and 45 minutes
Masala Tomato Lentil, 42
2 hours
Bayou Chicken & Sausage Gumbo, 68
Cool Cucumber Soup with Mint, 217
Hearty Beef Stew, 179
Sichuan Beef Noodle Soup, 73
Vietnamese Pho with Beef, 80
4 hours
Basic Chicken Stock, 230
8 hours and 30 minutes
Deep South Burgoo, 198
Cool Cucumber Soup with Mint, 217
corn
Alaskan King Crab & Sweet Corn Chowder, 154
Mexican Tortilla Soup, 106
Brunswick Stew, 180
California Vegetable Medley Soup, 22
Cantonese Chicken Chowder, 109
Caribbean Jerk Chicken Chowder, 110
cutting from cob, 29
Deep South Burgoo, 198
Heart-Healthy Vegetarian Chili, 193
Hearty Fresh Vegetable, 21
Maryland Crab Chowder, 153
Roasted Corn & Green Chili Chowder, 136
Spicy Mayan Chicken Enchilada, 104

Sweet Corn Chowder, 29
Tex Mex Turkey & Tomato Soup, 115
couscous
Israeli Eggplant Stew with Couscous, 199
Spicy African Fish Stew, 205
crab meat
Alaskan King Crab & Sweet Corn Chowder, 154
Classic She-Crab Soup, 165
Indonesian Crab Soup with Lemongrass, 164
Maryland Crab Chowder, 153
cream. See also milk.
Alaskan King Crab & Sweet Corn Chowder, 154
Cajun Crawfish Chowder, 158
Classic She-Crab Soup, 165
Cream of Spinach with Roasted Garlic Soup, 143
Creole Shrimp Bisque, 159
Divine Cream of Mushroom Soup, 132
Fresh Tomato & Basil Bisque, 51
Lobster Bisque, 126
Mulligatawny Soup, 55
Nantucket Oyster Stew, 149
New England Clam Chowder, 150
Roasted Butternut Squash Soup with Sage and Apple, 15
Roasted Corn & Green Chili Chowder, 136
Roasted Garlic Scape Bisque, 137
Savory Cream of Asparagus, 48
Smoked Salmon Stew, 185
Sun-Dried Tomato & Roasted Garlic Soup, 52
Cream of Potato & Leek Soup, 135
Cream of Spinach with Roasted Garlic Soup, 143
Creamy Chicken & Wild Rice Soup, 92
Creole Shrimp Bisque, 159
Cuban Black Bean Soup, 30
cucumbers
Chilled Melon Soup, 221
Chilled Tomato & Avocado Soup, 218
Cool Cucumber Soup with Mint, 217
Gazpacho Soup, 214
curry
Curried Shrimp Soup with Mango, 162
Masala Tomato Lentil, 42
Massaman Chicken Curry Stew, 204
Mulligatawny Soup, 55
Persian Lamb & Spinach Stew, 201
Thai Coconut Shrimp Curry, 188
West Indian Squash Sambar, 34

Deep South Burgoo, 198
Delicious Farro & Cannellini Bean Stew, 189
Divine Cream of Mushroom Soup, 132
duck
Duck Soup, 121
Tasmanian Duck Soup, 119
egg noodles
Classic Chicken Noodle Soup, 99
Roasted Turkey with Egg Noodle Soup, 113
eggplants
Israeli Eggplant Stew with Couscous, 199
Mediterranean Vegetable Soup, 25
8 hour and 30–minute cook time
Deep South Burgoo, 198
8 servings
Bayou Chicken & Sausage Gumbo, 68

Beer & Cheese with Smoked Bacon Soup, 131
Big Occasion Bouillabaisse, 161
Broccoli & White Cheddar Soup, 128
Brunswick Stew, 180
Curried Shrimp Soup with Mango, 162
Deep South Burgoo, 198
Duck Soup, 121
Hearty Beef Stew, 179
Mushroom Barley Soup, 16
Lobster Bisque, 126
Rosemary Chicken Dumpling Soup, 95
Spicy Mayan Chicken Enchilada, 104
Split-Pea Soup, 37
Vietnamese Pho with Beef, 80
Turkey Soup with Chorizo, Potatoes & Leeks, 120
fennel
    Big Occasion Bouillabaisse, 161
    Roasted Carrot & Fennel Soup, 43
    Tunisian Fish Chowder, 173
    Vegetable Soup, 59
    Yellow Split-Pea Soup with Fennel, 38
15–minute cook time
    Cold English Pea & Watercress Soup with Mint, 223
15–minute prep time
    Abalone Soup with Straw Mushrooms, Ginger & Rice Noodles,
        172
    Alaskan King Crab & Sweet Corn Chowder, 154
    Albondigas or Mexican Meatball Soup, 75
    Basic Beef Stock, 229
    Basic Chicken Stock, 230
    Basic Fish Stock, 231
    Basic Vegetable Stock, 228
    Beef Borscht, 76
    Cajun Crawfish Chowder, 158
    Chicken Fajita Stew, 208
    Cioppino Soup, 148
    Classic Chicken Noodle Soup, 99
    Classic She-Crab Soup, 165
    Cream of Spinach with Roasted Garlic Soup, 143
    Creamy Chicken & Wild Rice Soup, 92
    Creole Shrimp Bisque, 159
    Curried Shrimp Soup with Mango, 162
    Divine Cream of Mushroom Soup, 132
    Fresh Tomato & Basil Bisque, 51
    Green Bean & Zucchini Soup with Quinoa, 58
    Healthy Halibut Chowder, 157
    Heart-Healthy Vegetarian Chili, 193
    Hearty Fresh Vegetable, 21
    Indonesian Crab Soup with Lemongrass, 164
    Israeli Eggplant Stew with Couscous, 199
    Italian Wedding Soup, 71
    Lobster Bisque, 126
    Mediterranean Vegetable Soup, 25
    New England Clam Chowder, 150
    Persian Lamb & Spinach Stew, 201
    Red Bean Chicken Chili, 187
    Savory Cream of Asparagus, 48
    Seven Bean Mélange, 19
    Slow Cooker Jambalaya, 202
    Smoked Salmon Stew, 185
    Spicy African Fish Stew, 205
    Spicy Lentil & Lamb Sausage Stew, 66
    Spicy Mayan Chicken Enchilada, 104

Spring Shrimp Soba Noodle Soup, 171
Sunchoke Bisque with Roasted Sweet Peppers, 142
Sweet Corn Chowder, 29
Tasmanian Duck Soup, 119
Thai Coconut Shrimp Curry, 188
Vegetable Soup, 59
West Indian Squash Sambar, 33
White Bean & Escarole Soup, 34
Yellow Split-Pea Soup with Fennel, 38
50–minute cook time
    Chicken Fajita Stew, 208
    Delicious Farro & Cannellini Bean Stew, 189
    Roasted Tomato & Red Pepper Bisque, 138
    Sun-Dried Tomato & Roasted Garlic Soup, 52
Fire Roasted Vegetable Soup, 18
fish. See also seafood.
    Basic Fish Stock, 231
    Big Occasion Bouillabaisse, 161
    Cioppino Soup, 148
    Healthy Halibut Chowder, 157
    Spicy African Fish Stew, 205
    Sweet & Sour Fish Stew, 168
    Tunisian Fish Chowder, 173
fish stock
    Alaskan King Crab & Sweet Corn Chowder, 154
    Basic Fish Stock, 231
    Big Occasion Bouillabaisse, 161
    Cajun Crawfish Chowder, 158
    Cioppino Soup, 148
    Classic She-Crab Soup, 165
    Creole Shrimp Bisque, 159
    Curried Shrimp Soup with Mango, 162
    Healthy Halibut Chowder, 157
    Maryland Crab Chowder, 153
    Nantucket Oyster Stew, 149
    Smoked Salmon Stew, 185
    Spicy African Fish Stew, 205
    Sweet & Sour Fish Stew, 168
    Tunisian Fish Chowder, 173
40–minute cook time
    Beer & Cheese with Smoked Bacon Soup, 131
    Rosemary Chicken Dumpling Soup, 95
    North African Vegetable Soup, 26
40– to 45–minute cook time
    Broccoli & White Cheddar Soup, 128
    Fresh Tomato & Basil Bisque, 51
    West Indian Squash Sambar, 33
45–minute cook time
    Chickpea Chowder with Purslane & Leeks, 129
    Chipotle Sweet Potato Bisque, 133
    Chorizo & Sweet-Potato Stew, 182
    Creamy Chicken & Wild Rice Soup, 92
    Cuban Black Bean Soup, 30
    Duck Soup, 121
    Fire Roasted Vegetable Soup, 18
    Israeli Eggplant Stew with Couscous, 199
    Roasted Carrot & Fennel Soup, 43
    Roasted Corn & Green Chili Chowder, 136
    Roasted Turkey with Egg Noodle Soup, 113
    Rustic Cauliflower & Cabbage Chowder, 140
    Spicy African Fish Stew, 205
    Spicy Lentil & Lamb Sausage Stew, 66
    Spicy Mayan Chicken Enchilada, 104

Spicy Southwestern White Bean Soup, 32
Tomato Florentine Soup, 53
Turkey & Wild Mushroom Soup, 118
White Bean Turkey Chili, 196
Yellow Split-Pea Soup with Fennel, 38
4–hour cook time
Basic Chicken Stock, 230
4 servings
Albondigas or Mexican Meatball Soup, 75
Asian Pork & Glass Noodle Soup, 79
Bacon, Tomato & Cheddar Chowder, 67
Smoked Ham with Great Northern White Beans, 64
Cajun Crawfish Chowder, 158
Chilled Tomato & Avocado Soup, 218
Classic She-Crab Soup, 165
Cuban Black Bean Soup, 30
Hot & Sour Soup (Tom Yum), 167
Indonesian Crab Soup with Lemongrass, 164
Maryland Crab Chowder, 153
Mediterranean Vegetable Soup, 25
Nantucket Oyster Stew, 149
New England Clam Chowder, 150
North African Vegetable Soup, 26
Roasted Carrot & Ginger Bisque, 47
Roasted Chicken Florentine, 96
Savory Cream of Asparagus, 48
Slow Cooker Jambalaya, 202
Smoked Salmon Stew, 185
Spicy Beef with Ramen Noodle Soup, 82
Spicy Southwestern White Bean Soup, 32
Shrimp Soba Noodle Soup, 171
Stuffed Green Pepper Soup, 56
Sunchoke Bisque with Roasted Sweet Peppers, 142
Sweet & Sour Fish Stew, 168
Taco Soup, 84
Tasmanian Duck Soup, 119
Thai Coconut Shrimp Curry, 188
Tomato Florentine Soup, 53
Tortellini con Brodo, 100
Red Bean Chicken Chili, 187
4–6 servings
Beef Borscht, 76
Cantonese Chicken Chowder, 109
Caribbean Jerk Chicken Chowder, 110
Chicken Azteca, 105
Chipotle Sweet Potato Bisque, 133
Cock-a-leekie Stew, 184
Fire Roasted Vegetable Soup, 18
Gazpacho Soup, 214
Greek Avgolemono Soup, 117
Heart-Healthy Vegetarian Chili, 193
Hearty Fresh Vegetable, 21
Lentil Soup with Lemon, 41
Masala Tomato Lentil, 42
Massaman Chicken Curry Stew, 204
Mulligatawny Soup, 55
Pizza Lovers' Soup, 72
Poblano Chicken Chili, 195
Roasted Corn & Green Chili Chowder, 136
Roasted Turkey with Egg Noodle Soup, 113
Rustic Cauliflower & Cabbage Chowder, 140
Sichuan Beef Noodle Soup, 73
Sicilian Chicken Soup with Bowtie Pasta, 103

Spicy African Fish Stew, 205
Tex Mex Turkey & Tomato Soup, 115
Turkey & Wild Mushroom Soup, 114
West African Peanut Stew, 207
White Bean Turkey Chili, 196
Yellow Split-Pea Soup with Fennel, 38
Fresh Tomato & Basil Bisque, 51

garlic
Abalone Soup with Straw Mushrooms, Ginger & Rice Noodles, 172
Alamo Red, Pure Texas Beef Chili, 209
Alaskan King Crab & Sweet Corn Chowder, 154
Albondigas or Mexican Meatball Soup, 75
Asian Pork & Glass Noodle Soup, 79
Avocado & Artichoke Bisque, 141
Bacon, Tomato & Cheddar Chowder, 67
Basic Beef Stock, 229
Basic Chicken Stock, 230
Basic Fish Stock, 231
Basic Vegetable Stock, 228
Bayou Chicken & Sausage Gumbo, 68
Beef Borscht, 76
Beer & Cheese with Smoked Bacon Soup, 131
Birthday Soup, 44
Big Occasion Bouillabaisse, 161
Broccoli Rabe Soup with Lentils & Spring Onions, 57
Broccoli & White Cheddar Soup, 128
Brunswick Stew, 180
Cabbage & Smoked Sausage Stew, 181
Cajun Crawfish Chowder, 158
California Vegetable Medley Soup, 22
Cantonese Chicken Chowder, 109
Caribbean Jerk Chicken Chowder, 110
Chicken Azteca, 105
Chickpea Chowder with Purslane & Leeks, 129
Chilled Tomato & Avocado Soup, 218
Chipotle Sweet Potato Bisque, 133
Chorizo & Sweet-Potato Stew, 182
Classic Chicken Noodle Soup, 99
Chicken Fajita Stew, 208
Cioppino Soup, 148
Classic She-Crab Soup, 165
Cock-a-leekie Stew, 184
Cold English Pea & Watercress Soup with Mint, 223
Colorado Green Chili, 190
Cream of Potato & Leek Soup, 135
Cream of Spinach with Roasted Garlic Soup, 143
Creamy Chicken & Wild Rice Soup, 92
Creole Shrimp Bisque, 159
Cuban Black Bean Soup, 30
Curried Shrimp Soup with Mango, 162
Deep South Burgoo, 198
Delicious Farro & Cannellini Bean Stew, 189
Divine Cream of Mushroom Soup, 132
Duck Soup, 121
Fire Roasted Vegetable Soup, 18
Fresh Tomato & Basil Bisque, 51
Gazpacho Soup, 214
Greek Avgolemono Soup, 117
Green Bean & Zucchini Soup with Quinoa, 58
Healthy Halibut Chowder, 157
Heart-Healthy Vegetarian Chili, 193

Hearty Beef Stew, 179
Hearty Fresh Vegetable, 21
Hot & Sour Soup (Tom Yum), 167
Indonesian Crab Soup with Lemongrass, 164
Israeli Eggplant Stew with Couscous, 199
Italian Wedding Soup, 71
Lentil Soup with Lemon, 41
Lobster Bisque, 126
Maryland Crab Chowder, 153
Masala Tomato Lentil, 42
Massaman Chicken Curry Stew, 204
Mediterranean Vegetable Soup, 25
Mexican Tortilla Soup, 106
Mushroom Barley Soup, 16
Nantucket Oyster Stew, 149
New England Clam Chowder, 150
North African Vegetable Soup, 26
Old West Chicken Adobo, 108
Persian Lamb & Spinach Stew, 201
Pizza Lovers' Soup, 72
Red Bean Chicken Chili, 187
Roadhouse Beef Chili, 192
Roasted Butternut Squash Soup with Sage and Apple, 15
Roasted Carrot & Fennel Soup, 43
Roasted Carrot & Ginger Bisque, 47
Roasted Chicken Florentine, 96
Roasted Chicken Pot Pie Soup, 98
Roasted Chicken with Pesto & Pink Lentils, 118
Roasted Corn & Green Chili Chowder, 136
Roasted Garlic Scape Bisque, 137
Roasted Turkey with Egg Noodle Soup, 113
Rosemary Chicken Dumpling Soup, 95
Rustic Cauliflower & Cabbage Chowder, 140
Sausage & Barley Soup, 86
Savory Cream of Asparagus, 48
Seven Bean Mélange, 19
Sichuan Beef Noodle Soup, 73
Sicilian Chicken Soup with Bowtie Pasta, 103
Slow Cooker Jambalaya, 202
Smoked Ham with Great Northern White Beans, 64
Smoked Salmon Stew, 185
Southern Comfort Soup with Smoked Bacon & Collard Greens, 87
Spicy African Fish Stew, 205
Spicy Beef with Ramen Noodle Soup, 82
Spicy Lentil & Lamb Sausage Stew, 66
Spicy Mayan Chicken Enchilada, 104
Spicy Southwestern White Bean Soup, 32
Split-Pea Soup, 37
Spring Shrimp Soba Noodle Soup, 171
Stuffed Green Pepper Soup, 56
Sunchoke Bisque with Roasted Sweet Peppers, 142
Sun-Dried Tomato & Roasted Garlic Soup, 52
Sweet Corn Chowder, 29
Sweet & Sour Fish Stew, 168
Taco Soup, 84
Tasmanian Duck Soup, 119
Tex Mex Turkey & Tomato Soup, 115
Thai Coconut Shrimp Curry, 188
Tomato Florentine Soup, 53
Tomato Vegetable Soup, 222
Tortellini con Brodo, 100
Tunisian Fish Chowder, 173
Turkey Soup with Chorizo, Potatoes & Leeks, 120

Turkey & Wild Mushroom Soup, 114
Vegetable Soup, 59
West African Peanut Stew, 207
West Indian Squash Sambar, 33
White Bean & Escarole Soup, 34
White Bean Turkey Chili, 196
Yellow Split-Pea Soup with Fennel, 38
Gazpacho Soup, 214
ginger
Abalone Soup with Straw Mushrooms, Ginger & Rice Noodles, 172
Cantonese Chicken Chowder, 109
Chilled Melon Soup, 221
Curried Shrimp Soup with Mango, 162
Hot & Sour Soup (Tom Yum), 167
Indonesian Crab Soup with Lemongrass, 164
Israeli Eggplant Stew with Couscous, 199
Masala Tomato Lentil, 42
Massaman Chicken Curry Stew, 204
North African Vegetable Soup, 26
Roasted Carrot & Ginger Bisque, 47
Shrimp Soba Noodle Soup, 171
Sichuan Beef Noodle Soup, 73
Sweet & Sour Fish Stew, 168
Thai Coconut Shrimp Curry, 188
Vietnamese Pho with Beef, 80
West African Peanut Stew, 207
gluten-free recipes
Alaskan King Crab & Sweet Corn Chowder, 154
Albondigas or Mexican Meatball Soup, 75
Beef Borscht, 76
Big Occasion Bouillabaisse, 161
Birthday Soup, 44
Cabbage & Smoked Sausage Stew, 181
Cajun Crawfish Chowder, 158
Chicken Fajita Stew, 208
Chipotle Sweet Potato Bisque, 133
Chorizo & Sweet-Potato Stew, 182
Cioppino Soup, 148
Creole Shrimp Bisque, 159
Cuban Black Bean Soup, 30
Fresh Tomato & Basil Bisque, 51
Green Bean & Zucchini Soup with Quinoa, 58
Healthy Halibut Chowder, 157
Heart-Healthy Vegetarian Chili, 193
Indonesian Crab Soup with Lemongrass, 164
Lentil Soup with Lemon, 41
Maryland Crab Chowder, 153
Masala Tomato Lentil, 42
Mulligatawny Soup, 55
Nantucket Oyster Stew, 149
North African Vegetable Soup, 26
Persian Lamb & Spinach Stew, 201
Pizza Lovers' Soup, 72
Roasted Carrot & Fennel Soup, 43
Roasted Carrot & Ginger Bisque, 47
Roasted Corn & Green Chili Chowder, 136
Roasted Tomato & Red Pepper Bisque, 138
Rustic Cauliflower & Cabbage Chowder, 140
Slow Cooker Jambalaya, 202
Smoked Ham with Great Northern White Beans, 64
Southern Comfort Soup with Smoked Bacon & Collard Greens, 87
Spicy Lentil & Lamb Sausage Stew, 66

Spicy Southwestern White Bean Soup, 32
Sunchoke Bisque with Roasted Sweet Peppers, 142
Sun-Dried Tomato & Roasted Garlic Soup, 52
Taco Soup, 84
Vegetable Soup, 59
West African Peanut Stew, 207
West Indian Squash Sambar, 33
White Bean Turkey Chili, 196
Great Northern White Beans
    Smoked Ham with Great Northern White Beans, 64
    Spicy Southwestern White Bean Soup, 32
    White Bean & Escarole Soup, 34
    White Bean Turkey Chili, 196
Greek Avgolemono Soup, 117
Green Bean & Zucchini Soup with Quinoa, 58
green beans
    Deep South Burgoo, 198
    Hearty Fresh Vegetable, 21
    Roasted Chicken Pot Pie Soup, 98
green peppers
    Bayou Chicken & Sausage Gumbo, 68
    Cajun Crawfish Chowder, 158
    Creole Shrimp Bisque, 159
    Delicious Farro & Cannellini Bean Stew, 189
    Israeli Eggplant Stew with Couscous, 199
    Pizza Lovers' Soup, 72
    Slow Cooker Jambalaya, 202
    Spicy African Fish Stew, 205
    Stuffed Green Pepper Soup, 56
ground beef
    Albondigas or Mexican Meatball Soup, 75
    Italian Wedding Soup, 71
    Roadhouse Beef Chili, 192
    Stuffed Green Pepper Soup, 56
    Taco Soup, 84

halibut
    Cioppino Soup, 148
    Healthy Halibut Chowder, 157
ham
    Brunswick Stew, 180
    Chilled Tomato & Avocado Soup, 218
    Smoked Ham with Great Northern White Beans, 64
    Split-Pea Soup, 37
harissa
    North African Vegetable Soup, 26
    Spicy African Fish Stew, 205
    Tunisian Fish Chowder, 173
Healthy Halibut Chowder, 157
Heart-Healthy Vegetarian Chili, 193
Hearty Beef Stew, 179
Hearty Fresh Vegetable, 21
Hot & Sour Soup (Tom Yum), 167

Indonesian Crab Soup with Lemongrass, 164
Israeli Eggplant Stew with Couscous, 199
Italian sausage
    Pizza Lovers' Soup, 72
    Sausage & Barley Soup, 86
    Tomato Florentine Soup, 53
Italian Wedding Soup, 71

jalapeño peppers

Chilled Tomato & Avocado Soup, 218
Colorado Green Chili, 190
West Indian Squash Sambar, 33
kale
    Chickpea Chowder with Purslane & Leeks, 129
    Duck Soup, 121
    Vegetable Soup, 59
    White Bean & Escarole Soup, 34
kidney beans
    Heart-Healthy Vegetarian Chili, 193
    Roadhouse Beef Chili, 192
    Seven Bean Mélange, 19

lamb
    Deep South Burgoo, 198
    Persian Lamb & Spinach Stew, 201
    Spicy Lentil & Lamb Sausage Stew, 66
leeks
    Avocado & Artichoke Bisque, 141
    Big Occasion Bouillabaisse, 161
    Chickpea Chowder with Purslane & Leeks, 129
    Cock-a-leekie Stew, 184
    Cream of Potato & Leek Soup, 135
    Delicious Farro & Cannellini Bean Stew, 189
    Persian Lamb & Spinach Stew, 201
    Turkey Soup with Chorizo, Potatoes & Leeks, 120
lemongrass
    Asian Pork & Glass Noodle Soup, 79
    Curried Shrimp Soup with Mango, 162
    Hot & Sour Soup (Tom Yum), 167
    Indonesian Crab Soup with Lemongrass, 164
    Sweet & Sour Fish Stew, 168
lentils
    Broccoli Rabe Soup with Lentils & Spring Onions, 57
    Mulligatawny Soup, 55
    Lentil Soup with Lemon, 41
    Masala Tomato Lentil, 42
    Roasted Chicken with Pesto & Pink Lentils, 118
    Seven Bean Mélange, 19
    Spicy Lentil & Lamb Sausage Stew, 66
    West Indian Squash Sambar, 33
Lobster Bisque, 126

Maryland Crab Chowder, 153
Masala Tomato Lentil, 42
Massaman Chicken Curry Stew, 204
Mediterranean Vegetable Soup, 25
Mexican Tortilla Soup, 106
milk. *See also* cream.
    Beer & Cheese with Smoked Bacon Soup, 131
    Broccoli & White Cheddar Soup, 128
    California Vegetable Medley Soup, 22
    Classic She-Crab Soup, 165
    Cream of Potato & Leek Soup, 135
    Creamy Chicken & Wild Rice Soup, 92
    Healthy Halibut Chowder, 157
    Maryland Crab Chowder, 153
    Massaman Chicken Curry Stew, 204
    Nantucket Oyster Stew, 149
    Roasted Chicken Florentine, 96
    Savory Cream of Asparagus, 48
    Sweet Corn Chowder, 29
    Thai Coconut Shrimp Curry, 188

Mulligatawny Soup, 55
mushrooms
  Abalone Soup with Straw Mushrooms, Ginger & Rice Noodles, 172
  Basic Vegetable Stock, 228
  Divine Cream of Mushroom Soup, 132
  Duck Soup, 121
  Fire Roasted Vegetable Soup, 18
  Hot & Sour Soup (Tom Yum), 167
  Mediterranean Vegetable Soup, 25
  Mushroom Barley Soup, 16
  Sichuan Beef Noodle Soup, 73
  Turkey & Wild Mushroom Soup, 114
mussels
  Beef Borscht, 76
  Big Occasion Bouillabaisse, 161
  Cioppino Soup, 148
  Nantucket Oyster Stew, 149
  New England Clam Chowder, 150

Nantucket Oyster Stew, 149
New England Clam Chowder, 150
90–minute cook time. See 1 hour and 30-minute cook time.
noodles. See also pasta.
  Abalone Soup with Straw Mushrooms, Ginger & Rice Noodles, 172
  Asian Pork & Glass Noodle Soup, 79
  Cantonese Chicken Chowder, 109
  Roasted Turkey with Egg Noodle Soup, 113
  Spicy Beef with Ramen Noodle Soup, 82
  Shrimp Soba Noodle Soup, 171
  Vietnamese Pho with Beef, 80
  Turkey & Wild Mushroom Soup, 114
North African Vegetable Soup, 26

okra
  Bayou Chicken & Sausage Gumbo, 68
  Brunswick Stew, 180
  Old West Chicken Adobo, 108
Old West Chicken Adobo, 108
olives
  Mediterranean Vegetable Soup, 25
  Pizza Lovers' Soup, 72
1–hour cook time
  Basic Beef Stock, 229
  Basic Fish Stock, 231
  Basic Vegetable Stock, 228
  Big Occasion Bouillabaisse, 161
  Brunswick Stew, 180
  Caribbean Jerk Chicken Chowder, 110
  Chicken Azteca, 105
  Chilled Melon Soup, 221
  Chilled Tomato & Avocado Soup, 218
  Colorado Green Chili, 190
  Gazpacho Soup, 214
  Cock-a-leekie Stew, 184
  Persian Lamb & Spinach Stew, 201
  Poblano Chicken Chili, 195
  Southern Comfort Soup with Smoked Bacon & Collard Greens, 91
  Red Bean Chicken Chili, 187
1 hour and 15–minute cook time
  Roasted Chicken Pot Pie Soup, 98
  Smoked Ham with Great Northern White Beans, 64

1 hour and 30–minute cook time
  Alamo Red, Pure Texas Beef Chili, 209
  Abalone Soup with Straw Mushrooms, Ginger & Rice Noodles, 172
  Roasted Butternut Squash Soup with Sage and Apple, 15
  Roadhouse Beef Chili, 192
  Split-Pea Soup, 37
1 hour and 45–minute cook time
  Masala Tomato Lentil, 42
onions
  Albondigas or Mexican Meatball Soup, 75
  Asian Pork & Glass Noodle Soup, 79
  Basic Beef Stock, 229
  Basic Chicken Stock, 230
  Basic Fish Stock, 231
  Basic Vegetable Stock, 228
  Bayou Chicken & Sausage Gumbo, 68
  Beef Borscht, 76
  Beer & Cheese with Smoked Bacon Soup, 131
  Birthday Soup, 44
  Broccoli Rabe Soup with Lentils & Spring Onions, 57
  Broccoli & White Cheddar Soup, 128
  Brunswick Stew, 180
  Cabbage & Smoked Sausage Stew, 181
  Cajun Crawfish Chowder, 158
  California Vegetable Medley Soup, 22
  Chicken Azteca, 105
  Chicken Fajita Stew, 208
  Chilled Tomato & Avocado Soup, 218
  Chorizo & Sweet-Potato Stew, 182
  Cioppino Soup, 148
  Colorado Green Chili, 190
  Classic Chicken Noodle Soup, 99
  Cream of Spinach with Roasted Garlic Soup, 143
  Creamy Chicken & Wild Rice Soup, 92
  Cuban Black Bean Soup, 30
  Curried Shrimp Soup with Mango, 162
  Deep South Burgoo, 198
  Duck Soup, 121
  Fire Roasted Vegetable Soup, 18
  Fresh Tomato & Basil Bisque, 51
  Gazpacho Soup, 214
  Green Bean & Zucchini Soup with Quinoa, 58
  Heart-Healthy Vegetarian Chili, 193
  Hearty Beef Stew, 179
  Hearty Fresh Vegetable, 21
  Israeli Eggplant Stew with Couscous, 199
  Italian Wedding Soup, 71
  Lentil Soup with Lemon, 41
  Lobster Bisque, 126
  Masala Tomato Lentil, 42
  Massaman Chicken Curry Stew, 204
  Mediterranean Vegetable Soup, 25
  Mexican Tortilla Soup, 106
  Mulligatawny Soup, 55
  Mushroom Barley Soup, 16
  New England Clam Chowder, 150
  North African Vegetable Soup, 26
  Old West Chicken Adobo, 108
  Pizza Lovers' Soup, 72
  Poblano Chicken Chili, 195
  Red Bean Chicken Chili, 187
  Roadhouse Beef Chili, 192

Roasted Butternut Squash Soup with Sage and Apple, 15
Roasted Carrot & Fennel Soup, 43
Roasted Carrot & Ginger Bisque, 47
Roasted Chicken Florentine, 96
Roasted Chicken Pot Pie Soup, 98
Roasted Chicken with Pesto & Pink Lentils, 118
Roasted Corn & Green Chili Chowder, 136
Roasted Garlic Scape Bisque, 137
Roasted Tomato & Red Pepper Bisque, 138
Roasted Turkey with Egg Noodle Soup, 113
Rosemary Chicken Dumpling Soup, 95
Rustic Cauliflower & Cabbage Chowder, 140
Sausage & Barley Soup, 86
Seven Bean Mélange, 19
Sichuan Beef Noodle Soup, 73
Sicilian Chicken Soup with Bowtie Pasta, 103
Slow Cooker Jambalaya, 202
Smoked Ham with Great Northern White Beans, 64
Smoked Salmon Stew, 185
Southern Comfort Soup with Smoked Bacon & Collard Greens, 87
Spicy African Fish Stew, 205
Spicy Beef with Ramen Noodle Soup, 82
Spicy Lentil & Lamb Sausage Stew, 66
Spicy Mayan Chicken Enchilada, 104
Spicy Southwestern White Bean Soup, 32
Split-Pea Soup, 37
Spring Shrimp Soba Noodle Soup, 171
Stuffed Green Pepper Soup, 56
Sun-Dried Tomato & Roasted Garlic Soup, 52
Sweet Corn Chowder, 29
Tex Mex Turkey & Tomato Soup, 115
Thai Coconut Shrimp Curry, 188
Taco Soup, 84
Tomato Florentine Soup, 53
Tomato Vegetable Soup, 222
Tunisian Fish Chowder, 173
Turkey & Wild Mushroom Soup, 114
Vegetable Soup, 59
Vietnamese Pho with Beef, 80
West African Peanut Stew, 207
West Indian Squash Sambar, 33
White Bean & Escarole Soup, 34
White Bean Turkey Chili, 196
Yellow Split-Pea Soup with Fennel, 38
oranges
Chilled Melon Soup, 221
orzo pasta
Greek Avgolemono Soup, 117
Tomato Vegetable Soup, 222
oysters. *See* seafood.

Parmesan cheese
Italian Wedding Soup, 71
Pizza Lovers' Soup, 72
Roasted Chicken Florentine, 96
Roasted Chicken with Pesto & Pink Lentils, 118
Vegetable Soup, 59
parsnips
North African Vegetable Soup, 26
Vegetable Soup, 59
pasta. *See also* noodles.
Birthday Soup, 44
Fire Roasted Vegetable Soup, 18

Italian Wedding Soup, 71
Roasted Chicken Florentine, 96
Sicilian Chicken Soup with Bowtie Pasta, 103
Tomato Florentine Soup, 53
Tomato Vegetable Soup, 222
Tortellini con Brodo, 100
peas
Classic Chicken Noodle Soup, 99
Cold English Pea & Watercress Soup with Mint, 223
Hearty Beef Stew, 179
Maryland Crab Chowder, 153
Roasted Chicken Pot Pie Soup, 98
Smoked Salmon Stew, 185
Split-Pea Soup, 37
Yellow Split-Pea Soup with Fennel, 38
peppers
Caribbean Jerk Chicken Chowder, 110
Chicken Fajita Stew, 208
Chilled Tomato & Avocado Soup, 218
Chipotle Sweet Potato Bisque, 133
Colorado Green Chili, 190
Delicious Farro & Cannellini Bean Stew, 189
Gazpacho Soup, 214
Heart-Healthy Vegetarian Chili, 193
Hot & Sour Soup (Tom Yum), 167
Israeli Eggplant Stew with Couscous, 199
Roasted Corn & Green Chili Chowder, 136
Roasted Tomato & Red Pepper Bisque, 138
roasting, 30, 32
Slow Cooker Jambalaya, 202
Spicy African Fish Stew, 205
Sunchoke Bisque with Roasted Sweet Peppers, 142
Tex Mex Turkey & Tomato Soup, 115
Persian Lamb & Spinach Stew, 201
pinto beans
Colorado Green Chili, 190
Poblano Chicken Chili, 195
Seven Bean Mélange, 19
Taco Soup, 84
Pizza Lovers' Soup, 72
poblano peppers
Chicken Fajita Stew, 208
Colorado Green Chili, 190
Cuban Black Bean Soup, 30
Poblano Chicken Chili, 195
Roasted Corn & Green Chili Chowder, 136
Spicy Southwestern White Bean Soup, 32
pork
Asian Pork & Glass Noodle Soup, 79
Brunswick Stew, 180
Chilled Tomato & Avocado Soup, 218
Colorado Green Chili, 190
New England Clam Chowder, 150
Smoked Ham with Great Northern White Beans, 64
Split-Pea Soup, 37
potatoes
Alaskan King Crab & Sweet Corn Chowder, 154
Bacon, Tomato & Cheddar Chowder, 67
Birthday Soup, 44
Cabbage & Smoked Sausage Stew, 181
Cajun Crawfish Chowder, 158
Caribbean Jerk Chicken Chowder, 110
Chickpea Chowder with Purslane & Leeks, 129

Chipotle Sweet Potato Bisque, 133
Chorizo & Sweet-Potato Stew, 182
Cold English Pea & Watercress Soup with Mint, 223
Cream of Potato & Leek Soup, 135
Healthy Halibut Chowder, 157
Hearty Beef Stew, 179
Hearty Fresh Vegetable, 21
Maryland Crab Chowder, 153
Massaman Chicken Curry Stew, 204
Nantucket Oyster Stew, 149
New England Clam Chowder, 150
Roasted Carrot & Ginger Bisque, 47
Roasted Chicken Pot Pie Soup, 98
Roasted Corn & Green Chili Chowder, 136
Roasted Garlic Scape Bisque, 137
Rustic Cauliflower & Cabbage Chowder, 140
Smoked Salmon Stew, 185
Spicy African Fish Stew, 205
Sunchoke Bisque with Roasted Sweet Peppers, 142
Sweet Corn Chowder, 29
Tasmanian Duck Soup, 119
Tunisian Fish Chowder, 173
Turkey Soup with Chorizo, Potatoes & Leeks, 120
Turkey & Wild Mushroom Soup, 114
Vegetable Soup, 59
West African Peanut Stew, 207
prep time
    10 minutes
        Alamo Red, Pure Texas Beef Chili, 209
        Asian Pork & Glass Noodle Soup, 79
        Avocado & Artichoke Bisque, 141
        Bacon, Tomato & Cheddar Chowder, 67
        Birthday Soup, 44
        Broccoli Rabe Soup with Lentils & Spring Onions, 57
        Cabbage & Smoked Sausage Stew, 181
        California Vegetable Medley Soup, 22
        Cantonese Chicken Chowder, 109
        Caribbean Jerk Chicken Chowder, 110
        Chickpea Chowder with Purslane & Leeks, 129
        Chipotle Sweet Potato Bisque, 133
        Chorizo & Sweet-Potato Stew, 182
        Cold English Pea & Watercress Soup with Mint, 223
        Cuban Black Bean Soup, 30
        Greek Avgolemono Soup, 117
        Deep South Burgoo, 198
        Delicious Farro & Cannellini Bean Stew, 189
        Duck Soup, 121
        Fire Roasted Vegetable Soup, 18
        Hot & Sour Soup (Tom Yum), 167
        Lentil Soup with Lemon, 41
        Maryland Crab Chowder, 153
        Massaman Chicken Curry Stew, 204
        Mulligatawny Soup, 55
        Mushroom Barley Soup, 16
        Nantucket Oyster Stew, 149
        North African Vegetable Soup, 26
        Old West Chicken Adobo, 108
        Pizza Lovers' Soup, 72
        Roasted Carrot & Fennel Soup, 43
        Roasted Carrot & Ginger Bisque, 47
        Roasted Chicken Florentine, 96
        Roasted Garlic Scape Bisque, 137
        Roasted Tomato & Red Pepper Bisque, 138

Roasted Turkey with Egg Noodle Soup, 113
Sausage & Barley Soup, 86
Sicilian Chicken Soup with Bowtie Pasta, 103
Smoked Ham with Great Northern White Beans, 64
Southern Comfort Soup with Smoked Bacon & Collard Greens, 87
Spicy Beef with Ramen Noodle Soup, 82
Spicy Southwestern White Bean Soup, 32
Sun-Dried Tomato & Roasted Garlic Soup, 52
Sweet & Sour Fish Stew, 168
Taco Soup, 84
Tex Mex Turkey & Tomato Soup, 115
Tomato Vegetable Soup, 222
Tortellini con Brodo, 100
Turkey Soup with Chorizo, Potatoes & Leeks, 120
Turkey & Wild Mushroom Soup, 114
West African Peanut Stew, 207
15 minutes
    Abalone Soup with Straw Mushrooms, Ginger & Rice Noodles, 172
    Alaskan King Crab & Sweet Corn Chowder, 154
    Albondigas or Mexican Meatball Soup, 75
    Basic Beef Stock, 229
    Basic Chicken Stock, 230
    Basic Fish Stock, 231
    Basic Vegetable Stock, 228
    Beef Borscht, 76
    Cajun Crawfish Chowder, 158
    Chicken Fajita Stew, 208
    Cioppino Soup, 148
    Classic Chicken Noodle Soup, 99
    Classic She-Crab Soup, 165
    Cream of Spinach with Roasted Garlic Soup, 143
    Creamy Chicken & Wild Rice Soup, 92
    Creole Shrimp Bisque, 159
    Curried Shrimp Soup with Mango, 162
    Divine Cream of Mushroom Soup, 132
    Fresh Tomato & Basil Bisque, 51
    Green Bean & Zucchini Soup with Quinoa, 58
    Healthy Halibut Chowder, 157
    Heart-Healthy Vegetarian Chili, 193
    Hearty Fresh Vegetable, 21
    Indonesian Crab Soup with Lemongrass, 164
    Israeli Eggplant Stew with Couscous, 199
    Italian Wedding Soup, 71
    Lobster Bisque, 126
    Mediterranean Vegetable Soup, 25
    New England Clam Chowder, 150
    Persian Lamb & Spinach Stew, 201
    Red Bean Chicken Chili, 187
    Savory Cream of Asparagus, 48
    Seven Bean Mélange, 19
    Slow Cooker Jambalaya, 202
    Smoked Salmon Stew, 185
    Spicy African Fish Stew, 205
    Spicy Lentil & Lamb Sausage Stew, 66
    Spicy Mayan Chicken Enchilada, 104
    Shrimp Soba Noodle Soup, 171
    Sunchoke Bisque with Roasted Sweet Peppers, 142
    Sweet Corn Chowder, 29
    Tasmanian Duck Soup, 119
    Thai Coconut Shrimp Curry, 188
    Vegetable Soup, 59

West Indian Squash Sambar, 33
White Bean & Escarole Soup, 34
Yellow Split-Pea Soup with Fennel, 38
20 minutes
Mexican Tortilla Soup, 106
Beer & Cheese with Smoked Bacon Soup, 131
Broccoli & White Cheddar Soup, 128
Brunswick Stew, 180
Chicken Azteca, 105
Chilled Melon Soup, 221
Cock-a-leekie Stew, 184
Colorado Green Chili, 190
Cream of Potato & Leek Soup, 135
Hearty Beef Stew, 179
Masala Tomato Lentil, 42
Poblano Chicken Chili, 195
Roadhouse Beef Chili, 192
Roasted Chicken Pot Pie Soup, 98
Roasted Corn & Green Chili Chowder, 136
Rustic Cauliflower & Cabbage Chowder, 140
Sichuan Beef Noodle Soup, 73
Split-Pea Soup, 37
Stuffed Green Pepper Soup, 56
Tomato Florentine Soup, 53
Tunisian Fish Chowder, 173
White Bean Turkey Chili, 196
25 minutes
Albondigas or Mexican Meatball Soup, 75
Bayou Chicken & Sausage Gumbo, 68
Chilled Tomato & Avocado Soup, 218
Cool Cucumber Soup with Mint, 217
Gazpacho Soup, 214
Rosemary Chicken Dumpling Soup, 95
30 minutes
Big Occasion Bouillabaisse, 161
Roasted Butternut Squash Soup with Sage and Apple, 15
Vietnamese Pho with Beef, 80
Pure Texas Beef Chili, 209

red beans
Chicken Fajita Stew, 208
Red Bean Chicken Chili, 187
red peppers
Chicken Fajita Stew, 208
Fire Roasted Vegetable Soup, 18
Gazpacho Soup, 214
Mediterranean Vegetable Soup, 25
Roasted Tomato & Red Pepper Bisque, 138
Sunchoke Bisque with Roasted Sweet Peppers, 142
rice
Albondigas or Mexican Meatball Soup, 75
Bayou Chicken & Sausage Gumbo, 68
Chicken Azteca, 105
Chicken Fajita Stew, 208
Creamy Chicken & Wild Rice Soup, 92
Deep South Burgoo, 198
Greek Avgolemono Soup, 117
Massaman Chicken Curry Stew, 204
Mulligatawny Soup, 55
Slow Cooker Jambalaya, 202
Stuffed Green Pepper Soup, 56
Tomato Vegetable Soup, 222
Thai Coconut Shrimp Curry, 188

Turkey & Wild Mushroom Soup, 114
West African Peanut Stew, 207
rice noodles
Abalone Soup with Straw Mushrooms, Ginger & Rice Noodles, 172
Cantonese Chicken Chowder, 109
rice vermicelli
Asian Pork & Glass Noodle Soup, 79
Spicy Beef with Ramen Noodle Soup, 82
Vietnamese Pho with Beef, 80
Roadhouse Beef Chili, 192
Roasted Butternut Squash Soup with Sage and Apple, 15
Roasted Carrot & Fennel Soup, 43
Roasted Carrot & Ginger Bisque, 47
Roasted Chicken Florentine, 96
Roasted Chicken Pot Pie Soup, 98
Roasted Chicken with Pesto & Pink Lentils, 118
Roasted Corn & Green Chili Chowder, 136
Roasted Garlic Scape Bisque, 137
Roasted Tomato & Red Pepper Bisque, 138
Roasted Turkey with Egg Noodle Soup, 113
Roma tomatoes
Fresh Tomato & Basil Bisque, 51
Roasted Tomato & Red Pepper Bisque, 138
Stuffed Green Pepper Soup, 56
Rosemary Chicken Dumpling Soup, 95
Rouille, 161
Rustic Cauliflower & Cabbage Chowder, 140

Sausage & Barley Soup, 86
sausage
Bayou Chicken & Sausage Gumbo, 68
Brunswick Stew, 180
Cabbage & Smoked Sausage Stew, 181
Chorizo & Sweet-Potato Stew, 182
Pizza Lovers' Soup, 72
Sausage & Barley Soup, 86
Slow Cooker Jambalaya, 202
Spicy Lentil & Lamb Sausage Stew, 66
Tomato Florentine Soup, 53
Turkey Soup with Chorizo, Potatoes & Leeks, 120
Savory Cream of Asparagus, 48
scallions
Abalone Soup with Straw Mushrooms, Ginger & Rice Noodles, 172
Chilled Tomato & Avocado Soup, 218
Cool Cucumber Soup with Mint, 217
Vietnamese Pho with Beef, 80
seafood. *See also* fish.
Abalone Soup with Straw Mushrooms, Ginger & Rice Noodles, 172
Big Occasion Bouillabaisse, 161
Cioppino Soup, 148
Creole Shrimp Bisque, 159
Curried Shrimp Soup with Mango, 162
Healthy Halibut Chowder, 157
Hot & Sour Soup (Tom Yum), 167
Nantucket Oyster Stew, 149
New England Clam Chowder, 150
Slow Cooker Jambalaya, 202
Spring Shrimp Soba Noodle Soup, 171
Thai Coconut Shrimp Curry, 188
Tunisian Fish Chowder, 173

serrano peppers
    Colorado Green Chili, 190
    Spicy Southwestern White Bean Soup, 32
serving sizes
    4 servings
        Albondigas or Mexican Meatball Soup, 75
        Asian Pork & Glass Noodle Soup, 79
        Bacon, Tomato & Cheddar Chowder, 67
        Cajun Crawfish Chowder, 158
        Chilled Tomato & Avocado Soup, 218
        Classic She-Crab Soup, 165
        Cuban Black Bean Soup, 30
        Hot & Sour Soup (Tom Yum), 167
        Indonesian Crab Soup with Lemongrass, 164
        Maryland Crab Chowder, 153
        Mediterranean Vegetable Soup, 25
        Nantucket Oyster Stew, 149
        New England Clam Chowder, 150
        North African Vegetable Soup, 26
        Red Bean Chicken Chili, 187
        Roasted Carrot & Ginger Bisque, 47
        Roasted Chicken Florentine, 96
        Savory Cream of Asparagus, 48
        Slow Cooker Jambalaya, 202
        Smoked Ham with Great Northern White Beans, 64
        Smoked Salmon Stew, 185
        Spicy Beef with Ramen Noodle Soup, 82
        Spicy Southwestern White Bean Soup, 32
        Spring Shrimp Soba Noodle Soup, 171
        Stuffed Green Pepper Soup, 56
        Sunchoke Bisque with Roasted Sweet Peppers, 142
        Sweet & Sour Fish Stew, 168
        Tasmanian Duck Soup, 119
        Thai Coconut Shrimp Curry, 188
        Taco Soup, 84
        Tomato Florentine Soup, 53
        Tortellini con Brodo, 100
    4–6 servings
        Beef Borscht, 76
        Cantonese Chicken Chowder, 109
        Caribbean Jerk Chicken Chowder, 110
        Chicken Azteca, 105
        Chipotle Sweet Potato Bisque, 133
        Cock-a-leekie Stew, 184
        Gazpacho Soup, 214
        Greek Avgolemono Soup, 117
        Fire Roasted Vegetable Soup, 18
        Heart Healthy Vegetarian Chili, 193
        Hearty Fresh Vegetable, 21
        Lentil Soup with Lemon, 41
        Masala Tomato Lentil, 42
        Massaman Chicken Curry Stew, 204
        Mulligatawny Soup, 55
        Pizza Lovers' Soup, 72
        Poblano Chicken Chili, 195
        Roasted Corn & Green Chili Chowder, 136
        Roasted Turkey with Egg Noodle Soup, 113
        Rustic Cauliflower & Cabbage Chowder, 140
        Sichuan Beef Noodle Soup, 73
        Sicilian Chicken Soup with Bowtie Pasta, 103
        Spicy African Fish Stew, 205
        Tex Mex Turkey & Tomato Soup, 115
        Turkey & Wild Mushroom Soup, 114

        West African Peanut Stew, 207
        White Bean Turkey Chili, 196
        Yellow Split-Pea Soup with Fennel, 38
    6 servings
        Abalone Soup with Straw Mushrooms, Ginger & Rice Noodles, 172
        Alamo Red, Pure Texas Beef Chili, 209
        Alaskan King Crab & Sweet Corn Chowder, 154
        Avocado & Artichoke Bisque, 141
        Birthday Soup, 44
        Broccoli Rabe Soup with Lentils & Spring Onions, 57
        California Vegetable Medley Soup, 22
        Chicken Fajita Stew, 208
        Chickpea Chowder with Purslane & Leeks, 129
        Chilled Melon Soup, 221
        Cioppino Soup, 148
        Classic Chicken Noodle Soup, 99
        Cold English Pea & Watercress Soup with Mint, 223
        Cool Cucumber Soup with Mint, 217
        Cream of Potato & Leek Soup, 135
        Cream of Spinach with Roasted Garlic Soup, 143
        Creamy Chicken & Wild Rice Soup, 92
        Creole Shrimp Bisque, 159
        Delicious Farro & Cannellini Bean Stew, 189
        Divine Cream of Mushroom Soup, 132
        Fresh Tomato & Basil Bisque, 51
        Green Bean & Zucchini Soup with Quinoa, 58
        Israeli Eggplant Stew with Couscous, 199
        Italian Wedding Soup, 71
        Mexican Tortilla Soup, 106
        Mushroom Barley Soup, 16
        Roadhouse Beef Chili, 192
        Roasted Butternut Squash Soup with Sage and Apple, 15
        Roasted Carrot & Fennel Soup, 43
        Roasted Garlic Scape Bisque, 137
        Roasted Tomato & Red Pepper Bisque, 138
        Seven Bean Mélange, 19
        Sun-Dried Tomato & Roasted Garlic Soup, 52
        Sweet Corn Chowder, 29
        Tunisian Fish Chowder, 173
        Vegetable Soup, 59
        West Indian Squash Sambar, 33
        White Bean & Escarole Soup, 34
    6–8 servings
        Cabbage & Smoked Sausage Stew, 181
        Chorizo & Sweet-Potato Stew, 182
        Colorado Green Chili, 190
        Healthy Halibut Chowder, 157
        Old West Chicken Adobo, 108
        Persian Lamb & Spinach Stew, 201
        Roasted Chicken Pot Pie Soup, 98
        Sausage & Barley Soup, 86
        Southern Comfort Soup with Smoked Bacon & Collard Greens, 87
        Spicy Lentil & Lamb Sausage Stew, 66
        Tomato Vegetable Soup, 222
    8 servings
        Bayou Chicken & Sausage Gumbo, 68
        Beer & Cheese with Smoked Bacon Soup, 131
        Big Occasion Bouillabaisse, 161
        Broccoli & White Cheddar Soup, 128
        Brunswick Stew, 180
        Curried Shrimp Soup with Mango, 162

Deep South Burgoo, 198
Duck Soup, 121
Hearty Beef Stew, 179
Lobster Bisque, 126
Mushroom Barley Soup, 16
Rosemary Chicken Dumpling Soup, 95
Spicy Mayan Chicken Enchilada, 104
Split-Pea Soup, 37
Vietnamese Pho with Beef, 80
Turkey Soup with Chorizo, Potatoes & Leeks, 120
Seven Bean Mélange, 19
shallots
Alaskan King Crab & Sweet Corn Chowder, 154
Albondigas or Mexican Meatball Soup, 75
Bacon, Tomato & Cheddar Chowder, 67
Big Occasion Bouillabaisse, 161
Cantonese Chicken Chowder, 109
Caribbean Jerk Chicken Chowder, 110
Chipotle Sweet Potato Bisque, 133
Classic She-Crab Soup, 165
Cold English Pea & Watercress Soup with Mint, 223
Creole Shrimp Bisque, 159
Divine Cream of Mushroom Soup, 132
Fire Roasted Vegetable Soup, 18
Greek Avgolemono Soup, 117
Healthy Halibut Chowder, 157
Indonesian Crab Soup with Lemongrass, 164
Maryland Crab Chowder, 153
Nantucket Oyster Stew, 149
Savory Cream of Asparagus, 48
Sunchoke Bisque with Roasted Sweet Peppers, 142
Sweet & Sour Fish Stew, 168
Tasmanian Duck Soup, 119
Tortellini con Brodo, 100
shitake mushrooms
Mushroom Barley Soup, 16
Sichuan Beef Noodle Soup, 73
Turkey & Wild Mushroom Soup, 114
shrimp
Abalone Soup with Straw Mushrooms, Ginger & Rice Noodles, 172
Big Occasion Bouillabaisse, 161
Cioppino Soup, 148
Creole Shrimp Bisque, 159
Curried Shrimp Soup with Mango, 162
Hot & Sour Soup (Tom Yum), 167
Slow Cooker Jambalaya, 202
Shrimp Soba Noodle Soup, 171
Thai Coconut Shrimp Curry, 188
Sichuan Beef Noodle Soup, 73
Sicilian Chicken Soup with Bowtie Pasta, 103
sirloin
Italian Wedding Soup, 71
Stuffed Green Pepper Soup, 56
Vietnamese Pho with Beef, 80
6 servings
Abalone Soup with Straw Mushrooms, Ginger & Rice Noodles, 172
Alamo Red, Pure Texas Beef Chili, 209
Alaskan King Crab & Sweet Corn Chowder, 154
Avocado & Artichoke Bisque, 141
Birthday Soup, 44
Broccoli Rabe Soup with Lentils & Spring Onions, 57

California Vegetable Medley Soup, 22
Chicken Fajita Stew, 208
Chickpea Chowder with Purslane & Leeks, 129
Chilled Melon Soup, 221
Cioppino Soup, 148
Classic Chicken Noodle Soup, 99
Cold English Pea & Watercress Soup with Mint, 223
Cool Cucumber Soup with Mint, 217
Cream of Potato & Leek Soup, 135
Cream of Spinach with Roasted Garlic Soup, 143
Creamy Chicken & Wild Rice Soup, 92
Creole Shrimp Bisque, 159
Delicious Farro & Cannellini Bean Stew, 189
Divine Cream of Mushroom Soup, 132
Fresh Tomato & Basil Bisque, 51
Green Bean & Zucchini Soup with Quinoa, 58
Israeli Eggplant Stew with Couscous, 199
Italian Wedding Soup, 71
Mexican Tortilla Soup, 106
Roadhouse Beef Chili, 192
Roasted Butternut Squash Soup with Sage and Apple, 15
Roasted Carrot & Fennel Soup, 43
Roasted Garlic Scape Bisque, 137
Roasted Tomato & Red Pepper Bisque, 138
Seven Bean Mélange, 19
Sun-Dried Tomato & Roasted Garlic Soup, 52
Sweet Corn Chowder, 29
Tunisian Fish Chowder, 173
Vegetable Soup, 59
West Indian Squash Sambar, 33
White Bean & Escarole Soup, 34
6–8 servings
Cabbage & Smoked Sausage Stew, 181
Chorizo & Sweet-Potato Stew, 182
Colorado Green Chili, 190
Healthy Halibut Chowder, 157
Old West Chicken Adobo, 108
Persian Lamb & Spinach Stew, 201
Roasted Chicken Pot Pie Soup, 98
Sausage & Barley Soup, 86
Southern Comfort Soup with Smoked Bacon & Collard Greens, 87
Spicy Lentil & Lamb Sausage Stew, 66
Tomato Vegetable Soup, 222
slow-cooker recipes
Chicken Azteca, 105
Colorado Green Chili, 190
Deep South Burgoo, 198
Slow Cooker Jambalaya, 202
Smoked Ham with Great Northern White Beans, 64
Smoked Salmon Stew, 185
Southern Comfort Soup with Smoked Bacon & Collard Greens, 87
Spanish chorizo. *See* chorizo.
Spicy African Fish Stew, 205
Spicy Beef with Ramen Noodle Soup, 82
Spicy Lentil & Lamb Sausage Stew, 66
Spicy Mayan Chicken Enchilada, 104
Spicy Southwestern White Bean Soup, 32
spinach
Chickpea Chowder with Purslane & Leeks, 129
Cream of Spinach with Roasted Garlic Soup, 143
Italian Wedding Soup, 71
Persian Lamb & Spinach Stew, 201
Pizza Lovers' Soup, 72

Roasted Chicken Florentine, 96
Tomato Florentine Soup, 53
Split-Pea Soup, 37
Shrimp Soba Noodle Soup, 171
squash
Fire Roasted Vegetable Soup, 18
Mediterranean Vegetable Soup, 25
Roasted Butternut Squash Soup with Sage and Apple, 15
Tomato Vegetable Soup, 222
West Indian Squash Sambar, 33
Stuffed Green Pepper Soup, 56
substitutions
Abalone, 172
clam broth, 150
escarole, 34
harissa, 26
orzo pasta, 222
potatoes, 114
purslane, 129
soy protein, 193
spring onions, 57
summer squash
Fire Roasted Vegetable Soup, 18
Mediterranean Vegetable Soup, 25
Sunchoke Bisque with Roasted Sweet Peppers, 142
Sun-Dried Tomato & Roasted Garlic Soup, 52
Sweet Corn Chowder, 29
sweet potatoes
Chipotle Sweet Potato Bisque, 133
Chorizo & Sweet-Potato Stew, 182
North African Vegetable Soup, 26
Roasted Carrot & Ginger Bisque, 47
West African Peanut Stew, 207
Sweet & Sour Fish Stew, 168

Taco Soup, 84
Tasmanian Duck Soup, 119
10–minute prep time
Alamo Red, Pure Texas Beef Chili, 209
Asian Pork & Glass Noodle Soup, 79
Avocado & Artichoke Bisque, 141
Bacon, Tomato & Cheddar Chowder, 67
Birthday Soup, 44
Broccoli Rabe Soup with Lentils & Spring Onions, 57
Cabbage & Smoked Sausage Stew, 181
California Vegetable Medley Soup, 22
Cantonese Chicken Chowder, 109
Caribbean Jerk Chicken Chowder, 110
Chickpea Chowder with Purslane & Leeks, 129
Chipotle Sweet Potato Bisque, 133
Chorizo & Sweet-Potato Stew, 182
Cold English Pea & Watercress Soup with Mint, 223
Cuban Black Bean Soup, 30
Deep South Burgoo, 198
Delicious Farro & Cannellini Bean Stew, 189
Duck Soup, 121
Fire Roasted Vegetable Soup, 18
Greek Avgolemono Soup, 117
Hot & Sour Soup (Tom Yum), 167
Lentil Soup with Lemon, 41
Maryland Crab Chowder, 153
Massaman Chicken Curry Stew, 204
Mulligatawny Soup, 55

Mushroom Barley Soup, 16
Nantucket Oyster Stew, 149
North African Vegetable Soup, 26
Old West Chicken Adobo, 108
Pizza Lovers' Soup, 72
Roasted Carrot & Fennel Soup, 43
Roasted Carrot & Ginger Bisque, 47
Roasted Chicken Florentine, 96
Roasted Garlic Scape Bisque, 137
Roasted Tomato & Red Pepper Bisque, 138
Roasted Turkey with Egg Noodle Soup, 113
Sausage & Barley Soup, 86
Sicilian Chicken Soup with Bowtie Pasta, 103
Smoked Ham with Great Northern White Beans, 64
Southern Comfort Soup with Smoked Bacon & Collard Greens, 87
Spicy Beef with Ramen Noodle Soup, 82
Spicy Southwestern White Bean Soup, 32
Sun-Dried Tomato & Roasted Garlic Soup, 52
Sweet & Sour Fish Stew, 168
Taco Soup, 84
Tex Mex Turkey & Tomato Soup, 115
Tomato Vegetable Soup, 222
Tortellini con Brodo, 100
Turkey Soup with Chorizo, Potatoes & Leeks, 120
Turkey & Wild Mushroom Soup, 114
West African Peanut Stew, 207
Tex Mex Turkey & Tomato Soup, 115
Thai Coconut Shrimp Curry, 188
30–minute cook time
Alaskan King Crab & Sweet Corn Chowder, 154
Cantonese Chicken Chowder, 109
Cioppino Soup, 148
Classic Chicken Noodle Soup, 99
Classic She-Crab Soup, 165
Cream of Spinach with Roasted Garlic Soup, 143
Curried Shrimp Soup with Mango, 162
Green Bean & Zucchini Soup with Quinoa, 58
Heart Healthy Vegetarian Chili, 193
Hearty Fresh Vegetable, 21
Lentil Soup with Lemon, 41
Massaman Chicken Curry Stew, 204
Mexican Tortilla Soup, 106
Mushroom Barley Soup, 16
New England Clam Chowder, 150
Sausage & Barley Soup, 86
Savory Cream of Asparagus, 48
Seven Bean Mélange, 19
Slow Cooker Jambalaya, 202
Smoked Salmon Stew, 185
Sunchoke Bisque with Roasted Sweet Peppers, 142
Tasmanian Duck Soup, 119
Tunisian Fish Chowder, 173
Turkey Soup with Chorizo, Potatoes & Leeks, 120
West African Peanut Stew, 207
White Bean & Escarole Soup, 34
30–minute prep time
Big Occasion Bouillabaisse, 161
Roasted Butternut Squash Soup with Sage and Apple, 15
Vietnamese Pho with Beef, 80
35–minute cook time
Birthday Soup, 44
Cabbage & Smoked Sausage Stew, 181
California Vegetable Medley Soup, 22

Cream of Potato & Leek Soup, 135
Creole Shrimp Bisque, 159
Healthy Halibut Chowder, 157
Lobster Bisque, 126
Maryland Crab Chowder, 153
Mediterranean Vegetable Soup, 25
Nantucket Oyster Stew, 149
Roasted Carrot & Ginger Bisque, 47
Roasted Garlic Scape Bisque, 137
Stuffed Green Pepper Soup, 56
Sweet Corn Chowder, 29
Taco Soup, 84
tomatoes
    Albondigas or Mexican Meatball Soup, 75
    Bacon, Tomato & Cheddar Chowder, 67
    Basic Vegetable Stock, 228
    Birthday Soup, 44
    Big Occasion Bouillabaisse, 161
    Broccoli Rabe Soup with Lentils & Spring Onions, 57
    Brunswick Stew, 180
    Chicken Azteca, 105
    Chicken Fajita Stew, 208
    Chilled Tomato & Avocado Soup, 218
    Cioppino Soup, 148
    Classic She-Crab Soup, 165
    Deep South Burgoo, 198
    Delicious Farro & Cannellini Bean Stew, 189
    Duck Soup, 121
    Fire Roasted Vegetable Soup, 18
    Fresh Tomato & Basil Bisque, 51
    Gazpacho Soup, 214
    Green Bean & Zucchini Soup with Quinoa, 58
    Heart Healthy Vegetarian Chili, 193
    Hearty Beef Stew, 179
    Hearty Fresh Vegetable, 21
    Indonesian Crab Soup with Lemongrass, 164
    Israeli Eggplant Stew with Couscous, 199
    Lentil Soup with Lemon, 41
    Lobster Bisque, 126
    Masala Tomato Lentil, 42
    Mexican Tortilla Soup, 106
    North African Vegetable Soup, 26
    Old West Chicken Adobo, 108
    Pizza Lovers' Soup, 72
    Roadhouse Beef Chili, 192
    Roasted Tomato & Red Pepper Bisque, 138
    Rustic Cauliflower & Cabbage Chowder, 140
    Sausage & Barley Soup, 86
    Sicilian Chicken Soup with Bowtie Pasta, 103
    Southern Comfort Soup with Smoked Bacon & Collard Greens, 87
    Spicy African Fish Stew, 205
    Spicy Mayan Chicken Enchilada, 104
    Stuffed Green Pepper Soup, 56
    Tomato Vegetable Soup, 222
    Sun-Dried Tomato & Roasted Garlic Soup, 52
    Tasmanian Duck Soup, 119
    Tex Mex Turkey & Tomato Soup, 115
    Tomato Florentine Soup, 53
    Tunisian Fish Chowder, 173
    Turkey Soup with Chorizo, Potatoes & Leeks, 120
    Red Bean Chicken Chili, 187
    West African Peanut Stew, 207
  Tomato Florentine Soup, 53

Tomato Vegetable Soup, 222
tortellini
    Roasted Chicken Florentine, 96
    Tortellini con Brodo, 100
Tunisian Fish Chowder, 173
turkey
    Roasted Turkey with Egg Noodle Soup, 113
    Tex Mex Turkey & Tomato Soup, 115
    Turkey Soup with Chorizo, Potatoes & Leeks, 120
    Turkey & Wild Mushroom Soup, 114
    White Bean Turkey Chili, 196
20–minute cook time
    Greek Avgolemono Soup, 117
    Indonesian Crab Soup with Lemongrass, 164
    Mulligatawny Soup, 55
    Old West Chicken Adobo, 108
    Roasted Chicken Florentine, 96
    Spicy Beef with Ramen Noodle Soup, 82
    Tortellini con Brodo, 100
20–minute prep time
    Beer & Cheese with Smoked Bacon Soup, 131
    Broccoli & White Cheddar Soup, 128
    Brunswick Stew, 180
    Chicken Azteca, 105
    Chilled Melon Soup, 221
    Cock-a-leekie Stew, 184
    Colorado Green Chili, 190
    Cream of Potato & Leek Soup, 135
    Hearty Beef Stew, 179
    Masala Tomato Lentil, 42
    Mexican Tortilla Soup, 106
    Poblano Chicken Pueblo, 195
    Roadhouse Beef Chili, 192
    Roasted Chicken Pot Pie Soup, 98
    Roasted Corn & Green Chili Chowder, 136
    Rustic Cauliflower & Cabbage Chowder, 140
    Sichuan Beef Noodle Soup, 73
    Split-Pea Soup, 37
    Stuffed Green Pepper Soup, 56
    Tomato Florentine Soup, 53
    Tunisian Fish Chowder, 173
    White Bean Turkey Chili, 196
25–minute cook time
    Asian Pork & Glass Noodle Soup, 79
    Avocado & Artichoke Bisque, 141
    Bacon, Tomato & Cheddar Chowder, 67
    Broccoli Rabe Soup with Lentils & Spring Onions, 57
    Divine Cream of Mushroom Soup, 132
    Hot & Sour Soup (Tom Yum), 167
    Italian Wedding Soup, 71
    Pizza Lovers' Soup, 72
    Sicilian Chicken Soup with Bowtie Pasta, 103
    Shrimp Soba Noodle Soup, 171
    Tomato Vegetable Soup, 222
    Sweet & Sour Fish Stew, 168
    Taco Soup, 84
    Tex Mex Turkey & Tomato Soup, 115
    Thai Coconut Shrimp Curry, 188
25–minute prep time
    Albondigas or Mexican Meatball Soup, 75
    Bayou Chicken & Sausage Gumbo, 68
    Chilled Tomato & Avocado Soup, 218
    Cool Cucumber Soup with Mint, 217

Gazpacho Soup, 214
2–hour cook time
    Bayou Chicken & Sausage Gumbo, 68
    Cool Cucumber Soup with Mint, 217
    Hearty Beef Stew, 179
    Sichuan Beef Noodle Soup, 73
    Vietnamese Pho with Beef, 80

Vegan favorites
    Birthday Soup, 44
    Chipotle Sweet Potato Bisque, 133
    Cuban Black Bean Soup, 30
    Fire Roasted Vegetable Soup, 18
    Heart Healthy Vegetarian Chili, 193
    Hearty Fresh Vegetable, 21
    Lentil Soup with Lemon, 41
    Masala Tomato Lentil, 42
    Mushroom Barley Soup, 16
    North African Vegetable Soup, 26
    Roasted Carrot & Fennel Soup, 43
    Roasted Carrot & Ginger Bisque, 47
    Rustic Cauliflower & Cabbage Chowder, 140
    Seven Bean Mélange, 19
    Spicy Southwestern White Bean Soup, 32
    Vegetable Soup, 59
    West Indian Squash Sambar, 33
Vegetable Soup, 59
vegetable stock
    Avocado & Artichoke Bisque, 141
    Basic Vegetable Stock, 228
    Birthday Soup, 44
    Broccoli Rabe Soup with Lentils & Spring Onions, 57
    Broccoli & White Cheddar Soup, 128
    California Vegetable Medley Soup, 22
    Chickpea Chowder with Purslane & Leeks, 129
    Chipotle Sweet Potato Bisque, 133
    Cream of Spinach with Roasted Garlic Soup, 143
    Cuban Black Bean Soup, 30
    Delicious Farro & Cannellini Bean Stew, 189
    Fresh Tomato & Basil Bisque, 51
    Green Bean & Zucchini Soup with Quinoa, 58
    Heart Healthy Vegetarian Chili, 193
    Hearty Fresh Vegetable, 21
    Masala Tomato Lentil, 42
    Mediterranean Vegetable Soup, 25
    Mushroom Barley Soup, 16
    North African Vegetable Soup, 26
    Roasted Butternut Squash Soup with Sage and Apple, 15
    Roasted Carrot & Fennel Soup, 43
    Roasted Carrot & Ginger Bisque, 47
    Roasted Corn & Green Chili Chowder, 136
    Rustic Cauliflower & Cabbage Chowder, 140
    Savory Cream of Asparagus, 48
    Seven Bean Mélange, 19
    Spicy Southwestern White Bean Soup, 32
    Sunchoke Bisque with Roasted Sweet Peppers, 142
    Tomato Vegetable Soup, 222
    Vegetable Soup, 59
    West Indian Squash Sambar, 33
    White Bean & Escarole Soup, 34
    Yellow Split-Pea Soup with Fennel, 38
Vietnamese Pho with Beef, 80

West African Peanut Stew, 207
West Indian Squash Sambar, 33
White Bean & Escarole Soup, 34
White Bean Turkey Chili, 196
white fish
    Big Occasion Bouillabaisse, 161
    Cioppino Soup, 148
    Sweet & Sour Fish Stew, 168
    Tunisian Fish Chowder, 173
wine
    Alaskan King Crab & Sweet Corn Chowder, 154
    Basic Beef Stock, 229
    Basic Chicken Stock, 230
    Basic Fish Stock, 231
    Big Occasion Bouillabaisse, 161
    Cajun Crawfish Chowder, 158
    Cioppino Soup, 148
    Creole Shrimp Bisque, 159
    Healthy Halibut Chowder, 157
    Lobster Bisque, 126
    New England Clam Chowder, 150
    Sausage & Barley Soup, 86
    Smoked Salmon Stew, 185
    Turkey Soup with Chorizo, Potatoes & Leeks, 120

Yellow Split-Pea Soup with Fennel, 38
yogurt
    Chilled Melon Soup, 221
    Chorizo & Sweet-Potato Stew, 182
    Cool Cucumber Soup with Mint, 217
    Roasted Tomato & Red Pepper Bisque, 138
zucchini
    California Vegetable Medley Soup, 22
    Fire Roasted Vegetable Soup, 18
    Green Bean & Zucchini Soup with Quinoa, 58
    Heart-Healthy Vegetarian Chili, 193
    Hearty Fresh Vegetable, 21
    Israeli Eggplant Stew with Couscous, 199
    Lentil Soup with Lemon, 41